Multiemployer Plans

A Guide for New Trustees
Third Edition

Joseph A. Brislin

Multiemployer Plans

A Guide for New Trustees
Third Edition

International Foundation *if*®
OF EMPLOYEE BENEFIT PLANS
Education | Research | Leadership

The opinions expressed in this book are those of the authors. The International Foundation of Employee Benefit Plans disclaims responsibility for views expressed and statements made in books published by the Foundation.

Edited by Patricia A. Bonner, Ph.D., CEBS

Copies of this book may be obtained from:
Publications Department
International Foundation of Employee Benefit Plans
18700 W. Bluemound Road
Brookfield, WI 53045

Payment must accompany order.

Call (888) 334-3327, option 4, for price information or see www.ifebp.org/bookstore.

Published in 2014 by the International Foundation of Employee Benefit Plans, Inc.
©2014 International Foundation of Employee Benefit Plans, Inc.
All rights reserved.
Library of Congress Control Number: 2013956309
ISBN 978-0-89154-737-2
Printed in the United States of America

2.5M/114

Acknowledgments

The author wishes to thank the following people who assisted by providing technical information for this book:

Tom Seay, David Lee and Larry Beebe
Bond Beebe

R.V. Kuhns & Associates

Doug Holden
Milliman Inc.

Diana Pendell, Helen Sherman and Rita Sickler
Regence Blue Cross Blue Shield of Oregon

Mort Zalutsky
Zalutsky, Klarquist & Reinhart, P.C.

Eugene Burroughs
Prudential Asset Management Company, Inc.

Ron Grossmann
Stoel Rives LLP

Doug Toschi
Propel Insurance

Diane Clausen
Pharmaceutical Strategies Group

Dedication

A special dedication goes to my wife, Linda,
who provided encouragement to complete
the project and editing.

Table of Contents

About the Author

Joseph A. Brislin served 35 years as general counsel with Timber Operators Council, Inc., a forest products manufacturing employer association in Tigard, Oregon. He advised association members on all aspects of labor law and served as advisor and trustee to several health and welfare and pension funds in the forest products industry.

Prior to joining Timber Operators Council, he served as attorney with the law firm of Dezendorf, Spears, Lubersky & Campbell. Mr. Brislin is a graduate of Paul Smith's College, Paul Smith's, New York. He earned his B.S.F. and master's degrees at the University of Washington and received his J.D. degree from the University of Oregon School of Law. He served as president of the Joint Council of Presidents of the Western Pension Conference and president of its Port-

land Chapter. Mr. Brislin was a member of the Oregon State Bar's Insurance Committee and was secretary/treasurer of the Portland Chapter of the Western Pension Conference.

Mr. Brislin was a contributing author of three International Foundation publications: *Guide to Benefit Plan Administration, Trustee Handbook* and *A Guide to Better Employee Benefits Forms*. He authored *The WARN Act—A Manager's Compliance Guide to Workforce Reductions* published by BNA, *A Manager's Guide to the Americans with Disabilities Act* and *A Manager's Guide to the Family Medical Leave Act*, and contributed to *Labor Law in the Private Sector* published by the Oregon State Bar.

He promoted the educational goals of the International Foundation for many years, serving as author, speaker, moderator, membership booster, chair and member of various committees as well as a member of the Board of Directors. He served as Secretary, Treasurer, President-Elect then President of the International Foundation Board of Directors from 2002 to 2006.

In Memoriam

As Multiemployer Plans: A Guide for New Trustees, Third Edition *was about to go to press, Joe Brislin passed away. Staff and members of the International Foundation are deeply grateful to Joe for his dedication to the Foundation and the benefits industry. Joe volunteered in nearly every capacity from speaker to author to president of the International Foundation. He had a deep commitment to trustee education and was always thinking of new ways to educate trustees. He had countless ideas for its improvement. We thank Joe for gracing us with his knowledge and enthusiasm over the years. He will be missed.*

Introduction

Welcome to the world of multiemployer plans and ERISA.

As a new trustee, you have received an important honor and accepted a serious responsibility. The union or management organization that selected you to be a trustee has confidence in your abilities to carry out your fiduciary duties.

The purpose of this book is to provide you with an overview of both multiemployer health and welfare plans and pension plans, and to explain the important role trustees play in the management of multiemployer plans. This book also introduces many terms and concepts you will be expected to understand and act upon as a new trustee. Practical examples and tips are offered that will be helpful throughout your term as a trustee. More specifically, this guide:

- Provides an overview of how trustees are selected and reviews the fiduciary duties a new trustee assumes
- Explores some of the eligibility and benefit decisions trustees make
- Introduces the basic principles and concepts of how pension plans and health and welfare plans are funded and administered
- Identifies the roles of professional advisors in assisting and advising trustees in the performance of fiduciary duties
- Explains some key terms, laws and trust documents that a new trustee must understand.

A trustee must administer a multiemployer benefit plan in accordance with plan documents. Throughout this book you are advised to obtain copies of trust documents, trustee policies, administrative forms and reports from your plan's professionals. To get started, ask your plan administrator to provide you with the items listed in the trust documents checklist on page 101. Place these documents in a three-ring binder for easy reference.

As you read this guide, you will be given tips to help you understand and evaluate the provisions in your plan's documents. You will be encouraged to meet with each of the professionals associated with your plan and to ask them questions. With these persons, review your plan's documents, administrative forms and advisory reports. These conversations will help you understand the purpose of your plan, how it is funded and how benefits are provided to participants.

Education is an ongoing responsibility for a trustee. Governments enact new laws and regulations; industry economics have positive and negative cycles; the demographics of plan participants change over time; and new technology improves benefit services. Trustees must keep abreast of these developments and be able to respond to the changes. Whenever possible, take the opportunity to learn about new concepts, ideas and technology, and evaluate how they might improve the way your plan provides benefits and services to participants.

As a new trustee, you have an opportunity and responsibility to influence how employee benefits are provided to workers in your industry. Make the most of this opportunity. These employees and their families are depending on you to act on their behalf.

CHAPTER 1

Trustee Responsibility

The appointment to serve as a trustee of a multiemployer plan carries the responsibility to act as a fiduciary and to make prudent decisions. While serving as a trustee, you must remove your union or management hat and wear a fiduciary hat. The purpose of this chapter is to introduce you to how a multiemployer trust is established, and fiduciary responsibility. This chapter will address the following among other issues:

- What is a multiemployer or Taft-Hartley trust?
- Who are the trustees of a multiemployer plan?
- What is a trustee's fiduciary duty, and what laws require this duty?
- What is a prohibited transaction?
- What happens if a trustee breaches a fiduciary duty?
- What are the key documents and provisions regarding fiduciary duty?
- What trust policies are key to fiduciary duty?
- Who are the professionals that assist and advise plan trustees?
- What responsibilities can trustees delegate, and what is the delegation process?
- What type of insurance can trustees purchase to protect themselves?

What Is a Multiemployer or Taft-Hartley Trust?

The National Labor Relations Act of 1935, as amended by the Labor-Management Relations (Taft-Hartley) Act of 1947, permits a group of employers to contribute money into a joint trust fund if it is established for the sole and exclusive benefit of employees, their dependents and beneficiaries. The Act requires these conditions be met:

- Employer and any employee contributions must be held in trust for the purpose of providing these health and welfare benefits: medical or hospital care for an illness or accident, disability or sick pay, dental care, vision care, and death benefits.
- Similarly, there must be a trust fund established to hold contributions for pensions or annuities. Such a fund must be separate from any trust fund used to provide health and welfare benefits.
- Separate trust funds may also be established to receive contributions for vacation, holiday and severance pay, unemployment benefits, apprenticeship or other training, scholarships, child care or financial assistance for housing.
- The detailed basis for employer contribution payments to a trust fund must be specified in a written agreement.

- The employer and employees must be equally represented in the administration of the joint trust fund, with an established procedure to resolve a deadlock.

Normally, pooling the resources of many employers into one multiemployer trust for an industry or jurisdiction provides more cost-effective benefits and administration than each employer could provide separately. The multiemployer trust has more purchasing power, achieves administrative savings and spreads the risk of unfavorable claims experience over a larger number of people.

What Is the Required Written Agreement?

The written agreement required by the Taft-Hartley Act is normally a clause in a collective bargaining agreement that obligates the employer to participate in and contribute to the trust. Most multiemployer trusts also require a participating employer to sign a *trust participation agreement* that reaffirms the collective bargaining agreement.

The participation agreement requires the employer to abide by the terms and conditions of the trust document. It sets forth the obligations of the employer including the process and procedures for reporting eligible employees, and for making contributions to the trust fund. The participation agreement also provides for interest and penalties when the employer is delinquent.

If a multiemployer plan allows an employer to cover owners, supervisors or other non-bargaining unit employees in the plan, a signed participation agreement is mandatory. A signed participation agreement is also required if a

---

Tips for New Trustees

✔ Review the clause in the collective bargaining agreement binding the employer(s) to your trust.

✔ Review a copy of the participation agreement(s).

---

union office covers its officials and employees in a plan.

A trust document is required by the Employee Retirement Income Security Act of 1974 (ERISA). What the trust document must contain is explained on pages 7 and 8.

Who Are the Trustees?

As provided in the Taft-Hartley Act, a multiemployer health and welfare or pension trust must be jointly administered by an equal number of employer and employee representatives. The plan for most multiemployer trusts is jointly sponsored by a union, and an employer association or other group of employers. For example, in the West Coast forest products industry, the Bledsoe Health Trust is jointly sponsored by the Carpenters Industrial Council and the Timber Operators Council (TOC). The latter is an association of forest products employers.

The trust document must provide how many trustees the trust will have and how these trustees are appointed. Normally, the sponsoring union has the power to appoint the trustees representing the employees, and the employer sponsor (e.g., employer association) has the power to appoint the trustees representing the employers. It is not unusual, however, for a trust document to specify another selection method. If a regional union has several locals, the trust document may specify that each of the locals has the power to appoint a labor representative. A trust document might also provide that specific large employers in an industry have the power to each appoint a management trustee. If two trust funds merge, equal trustee representation from each of the merged entities may be required. No matter what the appointment method or how many trustees a plan has— The number of employee and employer representatives must be equal. Employers may not influence whom the union appoints, and the union may not influence whom management appoints.

The trust document must also define trustee terms of office, explain how a trustee is removed from serving a trust and establish a procedure for appointing a successor in the event a trustee dies or resigns. Normally, the trust agreement provides

Multiemployer Plans: A Guide for New Trustees

that the party who has the power to appoint a trustee also has the power to remove a trustee.

If a trustee commits a serious violation of the law, the federal government has the power to obtain a court order to remove a trustee and appoint a replacement.

Tips for New Trustees

✔ *In your trustee notebook, maintain an updated list of all the management and labor trustees, with their mail and e-mail addresses and telephone numbers. This list will be a handy reference.*

✔ *Review the provisions in the trust document regarding how trustees are appointed and how trustee meetings are conducted (e.g., who calls the meetings, quorum requirements, voting procedure). If you have any questions on procedure, ask your plan administrator.*

What Is a Trustee's Fiduciary Duty?

The Taft-Hartley Act requires trustees manage multiemployer health, welfare and pension trust plans for the exclusive purpose of providing benefits to participating employees, their dependents and beneficiaries. In addition, the Employee Retirement Income Security Act of 1974 (ERISA) places fiduciary obligations upon trustees to protect the interests of plan participants. ERISA covers all qualified multiemployer benefit plans with certain exceptions, such as public employee plans. Under ERISA, an *employee welfare benefit plan* is defined as any plan, fund or program providing medical, hospital or surgical benefits; sickness, disability, death, unemployment or vacation benefits; apprenticeship or other training program; dependent care; scholarship funds; or any benefit described in Section 302(c) of the Taft-Hartley Act. ERISA defines an *employee pension plan* as any plan, fund or program that provides retirement income to employees.

Every employee benefit plan covered by ERISA is subject to standards of fiduciary responsibility. A *plan fiduciary* is any person who:
- Has or exercises any discretionary authority or control over the management or administration of the plan
- Has any authority over the management or disposition of the plan's assets or
- Gives investment advice.

A trustee of a multiemployer health and welfare or pension plan normally meets all of the definitions of a fiduciary. Trustees normally establish the eligibility rules, set benefit levels, determine the procedures for the payment of benefits and develop guidelines for the investment of trust assets. Each of these functions constitutes discretionary control over the management and administration of the plan.

ERISA requires fiduciaries to discharge their duties solely in the interest of plan participants, their dependents and beneficiaries. The exclusive purpose of the fiduciary duty is to provide benefits and to defray reasonable expenses of plan administration. ERISA Section 404(a) requires a fiduciary to:
- Act with the care, skill, prudence and diligence under the circumstances then prevailing that a prudent person acting in a like capacity and familiar with such matters would use in the conduct of an enterprise of like character and with like aims
- Follow the documents and instruments governing the plan insofar as such documents and instruments are consistent with ERISA
- Diversify plan investments to minimize the risk of large losses, unless under the circumstances it is clearly prudent not to do so.

In summary, ERISA requires a trustee to be familiar with and understand the purpose of the plan and how it is administered. A trustee must also administer the plan in accordance with plan documents and applicable laws and regulations. A trustee must ensure his or her decisions are always in the best interest of plan participants and their dependents.

To Whom Must Trustees Be Loyal?

The Taft-Hartley Act requires a multiemployer plan to have an equal number of employer and employee representatives as trustees. Do labor and management representatives who wear union or employer hats when negotiating health and welfare or pension issues at the collective bargaining table have to give up their representative hat when they serve as trustees? In 1981 the United States Supreme Court answered this question when it issued its decision in *NLRB v. Amax Coal Company*. The Supreme Court held:

> Although [the Taft-Hartley Act] requires an equal balance between trustees appointed by the union and those appointed by the employer, nothing in the language of [the Taft-Hartley Act] reveals any congressional intent that a trustee should or may administer a trust fund in the interest of the party that appointed him. . . .
>
> Under the principles of equity, a trustee bears an unwavering duty to complete loyalty to the beneficiaries of the trust, to the exclusion of the interests of all other parties.
>
> [ERISA] imposes upon each trustee an affirmative duty to prevent every other trustee of the same fund from breaching fiduciary duties, including the duty to act solely on behalf of the beneficiary.

In summary, both labor and employer representatives must exchange their representative hats for fiduciary hats when they assume their role as trustees. This does not mean, however, that a trustee must disregard all of his or her union or employer connections. For example, if union members voice a strong preference for medical benefits over dental benefits at union meetings, the union trustees can consider this information and share it with employer trustees when making benefit design decisions for the trust. If employer trustees are aware of unfavorable economic conditions that will affect future employment levels, the employer trustees should consider this information and share it with union trustees when creating policy on plan eligibility and funding.

A union or management representative may retain his or her representative hat when bargaining—even if it affects the multiemployer plan. For example, the industry is suffering from unfavorable economic conditions that leads labor and management representatives to negotiate lower contributions for a health and welfare plan in a new collective bargaining agreement. Later acting as trustees, these same labor and management representatives may have to lower the benefit levels in the health and welfare plan due to the decrease in contribution income. In this situation, the labor and management representatives acted properly when wearing their representative hats at the collective bargaining table and later when wearing their trustee hats (see, e.g., *Evan v. Bixley*, 11th Circuit 1985).

What ERISA prohibits is placing a labor or employer agenda before the interests of plan participants when wearing the trustee hat. Consider a multiemployer plan that has sufficient funding to add orthodontic care to its dental benefits. The employer trustees cannot oppose adding orthodontic benefits to the multiemployer plan solely because the employer association's separate medical plan for salaried employees does not have an orthodontic benefit. The employer trustees also cannot act in their own self-interest because they will have a political and monetary problem if they give the new benefit to union employees but not to salaried employees. Employer trustees must remove their employer interest hat and act solely in the interests of the multiemployer plan participants and dependents.

How Are Trustee Deadlocks Resolved?

The labor trustees of a health and welfare plan want to accept a bid from Insurance Carrier A, but the management trustees believe Insurance Carrier B's bid is more desirable. There is a deadlock between the labor and management trustees, and the health and welfare plan needs an insurance carrier. How is this deadlock resolved?

The Taft-Hartley Act specifically provides that every multiemployer plan contain a provision in the trust agreement for compulsory arbitration when trustees deadlock. The written provision must specify how an arbitrator will be selected and that the arbitrator's decision is binding on all parties. The provision may provide that the cost of the arbitration be borne by the trust and paid with trust assets.

Because arbitration can be costly and time-consuming, trustees may desire another dispute resolution procedure. Some multiemployer plans hire a neutral trustee who attends all meetings. If the labor and management trustees deadlock, the decision of the neutral trustee resolves the deadlock.

Tips for New Trustees

✔ *Review the dispute resolution procedure in the trust document. Ask your plan administrator and attorney if any issue has ever been arbitrated and, if so, what were the results.*

What Is a Prohibited Transaction?

ERISA identifies specific transactions that a trustee may not engage in or permit to occur. The *prohibited transactions* identified in ERISA involve dealings between trustees and a party in interest. A *party in interest* is defined as plan administrators, officers, fiduciaries, trustees, custodians and legal counsel; trust employees; personnel providing services to the plan; participating employers and their employees, officers, directors, 10% shareholders; and unions whose members are covered by the plan, including union officers, directors and employees. A trustee cannot:

- Deal with assets of the plan in his or her own interest or account
- Act in a transaction with a party in interest if it is adverse to the interests of the plan or plan participants
- Receive any consideration for his or her personal account from any party in connection with a transaction involving the assets of the plan.

ERISA has specific exemptions to these prohibited transactions, and the Department of Labor has the authority to issue other exemptions. The ERISA-specific exemptions include:

- Loans made by a plan to parties in interest, if the loans are made available to all plan participants and dependents according to specific plan provisions, bear reasonable interest rates and are adequately secured
- Contracts made with a party in interest for office space or services (e.g., legal, accounting) necessary for the establishment or operation of the plan, if no more than reasonable compensation is paid
- Contracts for insurance or annuities with one or more insurers qualified to do business in the state, if reasonable compensation is paid.

The following are examples where the courts found multiemployer plan trustees committed a prohibited transaction or other breach of fiduciary duty:

- A multiemployer plan administrator breached his fiduciary duty by accepting contributions and paying benefits to a nonauthorized participant (*Iron Workers Welfare Fund v. Jefferson Davis Memorial Hospital* 1992).
- Trustees breached their fiduciary duty by paying the sponsoring union 8% of the contributions for administrative services performed by union business agents when there was no evidence the payment reflected the value of the services performed (*Dole v. Formica* 1991).
- Trustees breached their fiduciary duty by renting office space in a trust-owned building to the sponsoring union for $400 per month when market rates showed $600 was a more appropriate rental fee (*Dole v. Formica* 1991).
- Trustees breached their fiduciary duty by having the trust dental plan purchase benefits through an insurance carrier that paid a percentage of the premiums to a company owned by a trustee (*Brock v. Hendershott* 1988).
- Trustees violated their fiduciary duty when they authorized the fund to loan money to the union and made payments to union

officials for duties not associated with the fund (*McLaughlin v. Tomasso* 1988).

- Trustees violated their fiduciary duty by paying health care providers more than reasonable fees for services (*Sixty-Five Security Plan v. Blue Cross* 1984).
- Trustees who accepted free use of a boat from an insurance company selling insurance to the plan violated their fiduciary duty (*Donovan v. Tricario* 1984).
- Trustees who purchased insurance annuities without adequate knowledge of the insurance contract, competitive bids and benefit of expert advice breached their fiduciary duty (*Donovan v. Tricario* 1984).
- Employer trustees were held jointly liable for ratifying payments to union representatives without adequate records to show the services provided to the trust by the union representatives were necessary to the plan (*Kim v. Fujikawa* 1989).
- Trustees violated their fiduciary duty by making a $40 million loan to a participating employer without proper interest or security (*M & R Investment Co. v. Fitzsimmons* 1982).
- Trustees violated their fiduciary duty by authorizing monthly payments to themselves, although each one received a full salary from their union or employer (*Donovan v. Daugherty* 1982).
- Trustees breached their fiduciary duty when they purchased a jet aircraft using trust assets (*McDougal v. Donovan* 1982).
- Trustees breached their fiduciary duty when they invested virtually all of the fund's pension assets in a participating company (*Freund v. Marshal* 1979).

What Happens if a Fiduciary Duty Is Violated?

ERISA provides that any person who violates his or her fiduciary duty is personally liable for plan losses caused by the breach. A trust may purchase insurance for its trustees to cover liability or loss due to an act or omission by a fiduciary—as long as the insurance contract permits recourse by the insurer against the fiduciary.

✔ *Meet with your plan attorney and review how he or she ensures that trustees avoid prohibited transactions.*

An individual, union, employer or employer association (but not the trust) may separately purchase a rider from the insurance carrier that waives the insurer's right to recourse. This rider is called a *waiver of recourse.*

Fiduciary liability insurance does not cover a trustee for criminal acts, fraud, penalties, fines or punitive damages. ERISA requires trustees to be bonded. See page 14 for additional discussion on bonding and fiduciary insurance.

Is a Trustee Liable for the Acts of Others?

Many new trustees ask what happens if other trustees vote for an action that causes a breach of fiduciary duty, but the new trustee votes against it. If a trustee knows or should have known the other trustees committed a fiduciary breach of duty, that trustee is also liable. Casting a negative vote or abstaining from voting does not relieve the trustee from liability. The trustee must take prompt action such as reporting the breach to the U.S. Department of Labor or taking injunctive action in the U.S. District Court to be absolved from liability.

May a Trustee Receive Trust Fund Money?

A trustee may not receive any compensation from a trust for performing trustee duties if the trustee is receiving a wage or salary from a union or an employer. The trustee may, however, receive reimbursement for out-of-pocket expenses for performance of trustee duties. For example, Joan receives a salary from her local union and drives 300 miles to attend a one-day trust meeting. Her out-of-pocket expenses are $110 for a hotel room, $28 for dinner and $8.75 for breakfast. Joan may not receive any salary or wage from the trust for attending the trust meeting. Joan is, however, entitled to reimbursement from the trust for the $110 room, the $36.75 meal expenses and a reasonable mileage reimbursement as long as the union does not reimburse Joan for the same travel expenses. All expenses must be documented with proper receipts.

A trustee who is not paid by either the union or employer may be reimbursed for actual lost wages or salary for the time spent in the trust meeting. For example, a carpenter may be reimbursed the lost wages and benefits he or she would have earned working on a jobsite.

A trustee may also be reimbursed for reasonable educational expenses if the trust document provides for it and the education relates to the trustee's fiduciary duty. Educational expenses include travel, meals, lodging and registration expenditures. Many educational opportunities for trustees are provided over the Internet. The cost of these educational sessions may be reimbursed under the same trust policy.

Tips for New Trustees

✔ Ask your plan administrator for a copy of the reimbursement procedure for your trustee notebook.

✔ Ask your plan administrator about the trust policy on reimbursing trustees for attending educational conferences.

What Are the Key Trust Documents Regarding Fiduciary Duty?

ERISA requires every employee benefit plan be established and maintained pursuant to a written instrument. This instrument is commonly referred to as a *trust document* or *trust agreement*. The required items in this document are:
- ☐ A full description of the purpose of the trust
- ☐ A procedure for appointing trustees and their term of office
- ☐ Identification of the trustee(s) with the authority to control and manage the operation of the plan
- ☐ A procedure that permits trustees to allocate administrative responsibilities to fulfill the purpose of the plan
- ☐ A procedure to establish and carry out fund policy
- ☐ A provision for holding and investing trust assets
- ☐ A procedure for how trust business will be conducted (e.g., meetings, quorums, voting)
- ☐ A procedure for resolving a trustee deadlock
- ☐ A claims procedure as to how payments are made from plan assets (e.g., to pay reasonable expenses, benefit payments)
- ☐ A procedure for amending the plan and identification of the person(s) given the authority to amend the plan
- ☐ A procedure for terminating the trust that includes what circumstances will result in termination and what happens to trust assets. This provision is very important if a merger with another multiemployer plan is considered.

Optional items that trustees may place in the written trust instrument include:
- ☐ A procedure for employing persons (e.g., legal counsel, benefit consultants, actuary, account administrator) to advise trustees on fiduciary duties
- ☐ A procedure to appoint or employ an investment manager to manage plan assets, or an investment consultant to advise trustees on asset allocation and monitor the performance of the investment manager(s)
- ☐ A procedure for purchasing fiduciary liability insurance as permissible by ERISA
- ☐ A procedure for payment of trustee expenses connected to trust-related education and duties
- ☐ A full description of the powers of trustees (e.g., formulate administrative rules; enter into contracts and agreements to carry out the purpose of the plan; retain professional advisors; enter into, defend and settle legal proceedings; authorize the custodian to pay expenses; require employers to submit contribution reports)

- A full description of the powers of trustees to delegate and allocate responsibility and the procedure to do so (e.g., the trustees may delegate the responsibility to perform the required annual financial audit to the auditor)
- A procedure on withdrawal liability for employers withdrawing from a pension plan.

Tips for New Trustees

✔ *Review a copy of your trust agreement to learn how procedures are set forth for your plan.*

✔ *The trustee must administer a plan in accordance with trust documents. Make sure you follow procedures when making trust policies and decisions.*

The Collective Bargaining Agreement

As explained previously, employer participation in a Taft-Hartley multiemployer plan requires a written agreement. The written agreement requirement may be met by an article or clause in the collective bargaining agreement. Normally, the clause in the collective bargaining agreement requires the employer to participate in the trust and specifies the amount of the employer's contribution. The clause in the collective bargaining agreement may also obligate the employer to abide by the terms of the trust document, outline the contribution procedure and describe the penalties for failure to make timely contributions.

The Plan Document

While some multiemployer trusts incorporate the plan document into the trust document, others have a separate plan document. Generally, the plan document identifies the benefits provided by the plan, the eligibility requirements for employees and dependents to participate in the plan, and the procedures that eligible participants and dependents must follow to obtain benefits. The plan document must inform participants how to appeal a denial of benefits and provide them with their ERISA rights. Claim appeals are discussed on pages 85 and 86.

As long as it meets ERISA content requirements, a plan document may also serve as the *summary plan description (SPD)* that must be made available to participants and beneficiaries. The SPD is an easy-to-read statement describing the provisions and features of a benefit plan. The SPD for a pension plan might state that all employees who work under the collective bargaining agreement are eligible to participate in the pension plan. The annuity pension benefit is $60 per month per unit of credit. A unit of credit is defined as 1,000 hours worked per calendar year, and a participant is vested with five units of credit. A vested participant may apply for retirement at the age of 62 or older. Following the SPD, Jack, who is 62 years old and has five years of service (units of credit), may apply for a $300 per month annuity pension benefit (5 units of credit $\times$ $60 per unit).

Tips for New Trustees

✔ *Keep a current copy of the SPD in your trustee notebook.*

✔ *Review the SPD and become familiar with your plan's eligibility rules and benefit provisions.*

The Minutes of Trust Meetings

At each trust meeting, trustees conduct the business necessary to operate the plan. The minutes of meetings are records of the business decisions and policies established by plan trustees. For example, during a health and welfare trust meeting, trustees may agree to renew the contract with a dental insurance carrier for one year with a premium rate increase of 3%. Plan trustees may also decide that the maximum annual benefit for orthodontic care will be increased from $1,750 to $2,000 per year.

To carry out these decisions, the trustees direct their insurance consultant to enter into a one-year contract with the dental carrier on

✔ *Obtain copies of the minutes of trust meetings for at least the last two years from your plan administrator and review them.*

✔ *After each trust meeting, place the minutes in a file where they are accessible to you and keep the file up to date.*

✔ *If your review of the minutes raises any questions, ask the appropriate professional advisor for an answer.*

---

their behalf. The trustees may also direct the plan administrator to amend the plan document and summary plan description, and notify plan participants that there will be an increase in the maximum annual orthodontia benefit. The minutes of trust meetings are records of trustee decisions including who is responsible for putting these decisions into effect.

Trustees have a fiduciary duty to administer a plan in accordance with trust documents and the law. Meeting minutes are the official record that trustees followed the procedures required both by law and trust documents. Minutes also show that trustee actions were prudent. Trustees should be sure that all economic factors and professional advice influencing a decision are recorded in the minutes.

When trustees consider bids from multiple insurance carriers before renewing a contract, the minutes should reflect all of the financial comparisons, an evaluation of each vendor's ability to provide service, and other relevant data that distinguish the bids. The minutes should also reflect that trustees understood the differences in the bids and clearly explain why one carrier was chosen over the other(s). Minutes that simply state the trustees reviewed two or more bids and a motion was made, seconded and passed to select Carrier A are inadequate.

If either the Internal Revenue Service (IRS) or the U.S. Department of Labor (DOL) audits a multiemployer pension plan or health and wel-

fare plan, the processes used by the trustees in the performance of fiduciary duty are examined. The trust documents outline the processes the trustees must use to achieve the purpose of the plan. The minutes of trustee meetings are invaluable documents to show each and every step that trustees took to achieve plan objectives. The minutes and reports from professional advisors also show that the trustees continuously monitored the process.

The IRS Determination and Opinion Letters

For employers, a major advantage of an IRS-qualified employee benefit plan is that employer contributions are a tax-deductible business expense. A substantial advantage of qualified plans for employees is that contributions to these plans are not taxed as income when they are made. In addition, the investment earnings on trust assets are not taxable when they occur. Contributions to a pension trust fund and the earnings on this money are eventually taxed, but usually not until the plan participant receives the money as a retiree.

An IRS determination letter establishes that a pension plan qualifies for tax-exempt status under IRS rules. The IRS issues an opinion letter for a funded health and welfare plan. Once a plan is qualified, it must maintain its qualification. When trustees make certain amendments to a plan, the changes must be submitted to the IRS. The trust attorney advises trustees when an amendment has to have IRS approval. When amending a plan, it is important for trustees to abide by the amendment procedure in the trust document.

✔ *Obtain a copy of the IRS determination letter from your plan administrator and put it in your trustee notebook.*

✔ *Ask your plan administrator and attorney if your plan has been audited by the IRS or DOL and what the results were. In addition, ask their opinion on what the result would be if the IRS or DOL were to conduct an audit today.*

What Trustee Policies Are Key to Fiduciary Duty?

Benefit Policy

The benefit policy for a trust is dictated by law, trustee philosophy and, in some cases, a collective bargaining agreement. When benefit policy is established in a collective bargaining agreement, it is usually referred to as a *maintenance-of-benefits provision*. The labor agreement requires the employer to pay the contribution amount necessary to maintain the benefit(s). A maintenance-of-benefits provision might require employers to fund a pension plan that provides a $60 benefit per unit of pension credit. Another provision might require employers to fund a plan that pays 80% of health benefit costs. In these two maintenance-of-benefits examples, the trustees must manage the plan to provide the benefit levels dictated by the collective bargaining agreement, and the employer is required to provide the necessary funding.

In many multiemployer plans, the collective bargaining agreement only requires the employer to contribute a set amount to the plan. The trustees of the plan establish the benefit policy that can be funded by the contribution required. If the agreement establishes a health and welfare contribution of $5 per hour, trustees of the health and welfare plan must select benefits that can be supported by $5 per hour.

The law dictates some benefits. For example:

- The Uniformed Services Employment and Reemployment Rights Act (USERRA) of 1994 as amended requires a pension plan to give both vesting and benefit credit for time spent in military service if the military service caused a break in the employee's regular employment.
- The Family and Medical Leave Act (FMLA) of 1993 requires covered employers continue medical insurance coverage for an eligible employee who is on FMLA-qualified leave.
- The Affordable Care Act (ACA) of 2010 dictates many benefits for health plans.
- The Pension Protection Act (PPA) sets funding requirements for an underfunded defined benefit pension plan.

When a law dictates a benefit, trustees must amend their plan to comply regardless of the terms of the collective bargaining agreement and plan benefit policy. A plan attorney should advise trustees on the legal requirements that affect multiemployer benefit plans.

In most multiemployer plans, trustees have a benefit philosophy that has evolved over a number of years. This philosophy is normally recorded in the minutes of prior trust meetings or another document. For example, pension plan trustees may have established a philosophy many years ago that a disability retirement benefit should protect participants who become disabled before reaching retirement age. The trustees may have also decided that the maximum payment a retiree makes for retiree medical insurance will not exceed 50% of the actual premium cost. Both of these policy decisions should be recorded in a past set of minutes. The actual benefit that results from the trustees' philosophy is reflected in the summary plan description (SPD) and other plan documents.

A new trustee must become familiar with the benefit requirements and philosophy of the trust. These factors may dictate the actions of professional advisors. For example, if pension plan trustees want to protect disabled participants before they retire, the plan actuary must determine how much funding will be needed to do so. In some hazardous industries, the amount of funding necessary to provide a disability pension benefit may be very costly and adversely affect the level of assets available for funding early and normal retirement benefits.

Tips for New Trustees

✔ *Ask the trustee chairperson, administrator and professional advisors of your plan to explain trustee benefit philosophy including how it affects the plan and plan funding.*

✔ *Ask each professional advisor how plan benefit philosophy affects the advice and service he or she provides trustees.*

If trustees want to keep retiree health insurance payments at 50% of the premium cost, the insurance advisor must prescribe what funding will accomplish this objective. In a declining industry, the cost to fund retiree medical coverage with only a 50% retiree self-payment may be substantial and affect the overall funding of the plan.

Collection Policy

ERISA assigns fiduciary responsibility for plan funding to plan trustees. If an employer is delinquent in making contributions, trustees have a duty to collect what is owed plus interest. If trustees do not actively seek collection, they commit an ERISA-prohibited transaction because they are lending money to a party in interest (see page 5 for more information on prohibited transactions). DOL regulations require trustees to establish and implement collection procedures that are reasonable, diligent and systematic to avoid a prohibited transaction under ERISA.

A written collection policy establishes the procedure trustees must follow to collect delinquent contributions. This policy typically states who is responsible for each step in the process and the time limits to accomplish each step. For example, a collection procedure may say that if an employer misses the normal contribution payment date on the tenth of the month, the administrator will send a registered letter to the delinquent employer on the 11th, demanding payment by the 16th. If the employer does not respond by the 16th, the plan attorney will write a letter to the delinquent employer demanding payment by the 25th. If the employer does not respond by the 25th, the plan attorney will file court action to enforce collection.

The trust agreement and collection policy must impose interest for late payments. Trustees may also impose penalty payments (e.g., liquidated damages and attorney fees) if the employer fails to make a timely payment. When collection requires the services of the plan auditor, trustees may require the delinquent employer pay the auditor fees as well.

Usually, a multiemployer plan conducts random payroll audits of a reasonable number of

✔ Review the written collection procedure in your trustee notebook. Ask your plan administrator and legal counsel to review the steps in the procedure.

✔ Ask your plan administrator what the common delinquency problems are and what is done to eliminate or reduce these problems. For example, what is the administrator doing to deal with employers that fail to make contributions on part-time and temporary employees who are performing bargaining unit work?

✔ While there may appear to be a good reason to make an exception to the collection procedure when there is a delinquency, do not permit them. Follow procedures and act on the advice of the plan attorney. See question 2 on page 16 for an example of a dilemma that trustees might face in pursuing collection and how to handle it.

employers every year to assure compliance with the contribution requirements. The authority of trustees to conduct random audits and the employer's obligation to comply with an audit request is set forth in the trust document and the participation agreement. The trust usually bears the cost of the random audit. The collection policy, however, may provide that the employer bears the full or prorated audit costs plus interest and penalties when a delinquency is found during an audit.

The trustee duty to collect also applies to debts owed by participants. Consider a surviving spouse who did not report the death of a retiree and continued to collect full pension payments, or a participant who collected short-term disability payments from a health and welfare trust while working outside the industry. Trustees must determine the amount owed the trust and seek collection.

It is important to keep in mind that ERISA does not require trustees to expend trust funds to pursue an uncollectible or doubtful delinquency claim. The written collection procedure, therefore, should establish guidelines on when trustees have the authority to settle a claim for less than the full amount owed. Before any settlement is entered into, trustees should be fully advised by the plan attorney. The minutes of the trust meeting should fully explain the attorney's advice and set forth the facts that the trustees relied on to make their settlement decision.

Investment Policy
See Chapter 4.

Communication With Participants
A multiemployer benefit plan may provide the highest level of benefits and be the best funded in the entire country, but it does not serve its purpose if participants do not understand how the plan works and how to obtain plan benefits. An important fiduciary duty for trustees is to communicate with participants and their dependents. ERISA requires the following minimum communication with plan participants:

- A copy of the **summary plan description** must be provided to all participants. The SPD must be written in a manner that can be understood by the average plan participant. The SPD informs participants of their rights and obligations, eligibility rules, circumstances under which benefits will be denied, how to file for benefits and how to appeal a claim denial. If a significant number of participants speak a language other than English, the plan must provide the SPD in this other language.
- A **summary annual report** must be provided annually to all participants to inform them of the financial status of the plan.
- A **summary of material modification** explains any significant amendments or changes to the plan. It is sent to participants only when necessary.
- A **benefits statement** must be provided to pension participants once a year upon request and to any vested participant upon termination. Many multiemployer pension plans provide an annual benefit statement to all participants once a year. The docu-

ment informs each participant of his or her current status in the plan and what benefits he or she is entitled to at normal retirement age.
- If a benefit is denied, the plan must send the participant a clear, written explanation of why the claim was denied; refer the individual to the provisions in the plan documents that the denial is based upon; and, if possible, explain what the participant must do to be eligible. For example, the normal retirement age is 65, and a 60-year-old participant applies for normal retirement. The administrator must tell the participant why his application was denied and explain how to apply for early retirement or reapply for normal retirement at the age of 65. Additional information on claim appeals is on pages 85 and 86.
- When a married participant wants to retire, the pension plan must provide the person with a joint and survivor notification and the spousal consent forms for the couple to make their pension election. See page 48 for a discussion of joint and survivor option.
- If a multiemployer pension or health and welfare plan will terminate, participants must be notified of the termination.
- If a plan is submitting a determination application to IRS, the plan must notify participants.
- If any participant wants a copy of plan documents (e.g., trust document, SPD, actuarial report), the plan must provide them to the participant. Failure to do so may result in monetary penalties.

There are several other communications required by law. Among these are COBRA notices (see question 3 on page 32), notices under the Uniformed Services Employment and Reemployment Act (USERRA) and notices required by the Pension Protection Act of 2006. The Affordable Care Act (ACA) requires a summary of benefits and coverage (SBC) be given to each person when he or she is first eligible to enroll in the health plan, during open enrollment periods and upon request. The plan attorney and administrator will inform trustees of these and other new notice requirements.

Who Are Plan Advisors?

ERISA permits and encourages trustees to engage the expertise of professionals to provide assistance and advice in the performance of fiduciary duties. Most trustees do not possess the expertise or experience in legal affairs, investments, plan administration, insurance underwriting, auditing and other specialized areas necessary to carry out the purpose of a trust. Trustees, therefore, exercise fiduciary prudence by utilizing the services of professionals who possess the desired expertise.

The trust document must contain a provision that gives trustees authority to retain professional advisors and to pay reasonable compensation from plan assets for these services. The trust document should also contain a provision on the delegation of responsibility and set forth the procedure that trustees use to make the delegation. When trustees delegate responsibility to a third party, they are relieved of the responsibility of any fiduciary breach by the third party as long as the delegation is proper and the trustees monitor the performance of the third party.

When trustees select a professional advisor, proper delegation involves making sure the professional is knowledgeable, experienced and competent in his or her area of expertise. Trustees must

also ensure the person has the proper qualifications and professional license or certification. The person should have the required bonding as well as errors and omissions (E&O) insurance coverage. The trust attorney can advise trustees on any legal requirements that professionals must meet. The attorney should also advise trustees on the desirability of having a contract with each professional advisor. Other chapters of this book offer discussion and tips on monitoring the performance of professional advisors.

Multiemployer plan trustees normally delegate responsibility for a number of trust duties to professionals. The following professionals are those commonly used. While some advisors are used by health and welfare as well as pension plans, other advisors are a unique need of one or the other type of plan. Additional types of professionals may also be employed by trustees when deemed necessary.

Actuary

An *actuary* gathers data and makes calculations that help trustees make financial decisions. An actuary also performs annual actuarial functions required by law for pension plans. See page 44 for more information on the role of the actuary for defined benefit pension plans.

Administrator

A third-party or salaried administrator performs the day-to-day administrative functions of a fund. See Chapter 5 for a complete discussion of the administrator's role.

Attorney

The plan attorney advises trustees on all legal issues, laws and regulations. The attorney, with the assistance of the administrator and consultants, can prepare plan documents, ensure the plan meets IRS qualifications and make filings required by law.

Auditor

An auditor performs the annual audit required by law and payroll audits of employer records to ensure contributions required by collective bargaining agreements are being made. See Chapter 6 for a discussion of the financial audit and the auditor's role.

Tips for New Trustees

✔ *Obtain the names, mail and e-mail addresses, and phone numbers for all of your plan's professionals. Keep the list in your trustee notebook.*

✔ *The professional advisors that work for plan trustees are **only** advisors. As a trustee you have the ultimate fiduciary responsibility to establish trust policy, eligibility rules and plan design. If a professional advisor attempts to dictate plan policy, be polite but firm reminding the advisor that he or she is exceeding the advisory role.*

✔ *See page 103 for tips on meeting with plan professionals.*

Custodian Bank

The *custodian bank* is the depository for plan premiums and contributions. A checking account at the bank is used to pay trust expenses. The custodian bank may also have physical custody of plan assets (e.g., stock and bond certificates, mortgage papers), collect and deposit dividends, and invest payments.

Insurance Carrier or Underwriter

An insurance company provides liability insurance coverage for trustees. Health and welfare plans also use an insurance company (e.g., Blue Cross, Prudential, Providence), a health maintenance organization (HMO) or a preferred provider organization (PPO) to provide medical insurance coverage and medical services to participants. See page 28 for more information on the role of insurers in health and welfare plans.

Insurance Consultant or Broker

An insurance consultant advises trustees on insurance contracts, underwriting, benefit design and monitoring claim performance. The role of insurance consultants and brokers in health and welfare plans is discussed in more detail on page 29.

Investment Manager and Investment Consultant

An *investment manager* manages and invests plan assets. An *investment consultant* assists trustees in asset allocation—selecting competent investment managers and monitoring their performance. See Chapter 4 for a discussion of managing trust investments.

What Is the Purpose of Bonding and Fiduciary Insurance?

ERISA requires trustees, plan fiduciaries and any other persons who handle plan assets to be bonded. A bond protects the trust from fiduciary breaches such as theft and the misappropriation of funds. The bond must be for 10% of trust assets up to a maximum of $500,000. The cost of a bond may be paid using trust assets.

As stated in prior sections of this chapter, trustees may also be personally liable for breaches of fiduciary duty. Fiduciary liability insurance protects trustees from personal loss. Even if trustees have not committed a fiduciary breach, there is the possibility that a plan and trustees may need a defense if sued by plan participants or a government enforcement agency. A primary purpose of fiduciary liability insurance, therefore, is covering legal defense costs.

The authority to purchase fiduciary liability insurance should be in the trust document. ERISA authorizes trustees to use plan assets to purchase this insurance if the liability insurance contract permits recourse against the trustee by the insurance company. Trustees, however, may personally purchase waiver of recourse coverage. In the typical multiemployer plan, trustees use plan assets to obtain fiduciary liability insurance coverage, and either the trustee or union and employer association purchase the waiver of recourse policy. Fiduciary insurance does not protect trustees from criminal penalties, fines, punitive damages, libel, slander or fraud.

The following is an overview and checklist of what trustees should consider when obtaining a fiduciary liability policy:

☐ Who is insured? What is the definition of *insured?* Does coverage include past as well as current trustees? A trustee should be assured that he or she will continue to be covered by the policy after his or her term as trustee ends. Is the coverage automatically extended to new trustees?

☐ Is the liability coverage for one fund or for several funds (e.g., health and welfare plan, pension plan, vacation plan, apprenticeship plan) if a trustee serves on several industry multiemployer plans? Are policy limits for the individual plans or for all plans combined?

☐ Are other persons besides trustees covered such as the plan administrator? If so, how does this affect policy limits and protection for the trustees? For example, can the maximum protection be used by the administrator—leaving no protection for the trustees?

☐ What acts are covered? Does the policy include legal defense and settlement costs? What is the definition of a *wrongful act?*

- [ ] What damages are covered and what is excluded? Normally, fiduciary liability insurance will not cover fines, penalties, taxes, punitive or exemplary damages; fraud, dishonesty or embezzlement; and libel, slander or criminal conduct.

- [ ] Is it a *claims-made* policy covering both past and current acts of trustees as long as the claim is made during the policy period? How is a dispute over coverage settled? For example, what happens if the insurance company alleges an act is not covered by the policy, but the trustees believe the act is covered?

- [ ] What information must trustees provide to the insurance carrier? Most policies exclude coverage if trustees have knowledge or could reasonably foresee a claim. What does plan counsel advise on providing information to the insurance company?

- [ ] What is the policy deductible? What are the policy limits? What is the premium? How is the decision on each of these made?

- [ ] What is the policy period (e.g., one year, two years)?

- [ ] How can the policy be canceled? What is the notice period? Is there a guaranteed renewable feature or is the policy contracted year by year? Who is responsible for keeping trustees informed of the carrier's intentions to renew?

- [ ] Who is responsible for renewals, check underwriting, and seeking other coverage and premium alternatives? Who is responsible for keeping trustees informed on these matters?

Tips for New Trustees

✔ *Ask your plan administrator to provide a copy of your plan's fiduciary liability insurance policy and put the copy in your trustee notebook.*

✔ *Ask the professional advisor who obtained fiduciary liability coverage for your plan to answer the questions listed above. Determine whether the policy has a waiver-of-recourse provision and who pays the premiums.*

Common Questions and Answers

1. Do the trustees or collective bargaining parties set the contribution rates and benefit levels?

In a typical multiemployer trust arrangement, the collective bargaining parties establish the contribution rate, and the trustees establish the benefits that the contributions will support. In some industries, however, the collective bargaining parties may also set benefit levels. If the collective bargaining parties do direct benefit levels, the plan trustees still have the fiduciary responsibility to properly fund the plan.

It is important for trustees and collective bargaining parties to communicate and set realistic expectations. For example, if the collective bargaining parties want to increase pension benefits from $50 to $60 per unit of credit in a new labor contract, they will need to understand the consequences of their decision on plan assets, as well as the level of employer contribution necessary to fund the $10 increase.

Neither collective bargaining parties nor trustees want to have a political and financial problem in which a collective bargaining agreement directs a benefit level, but the plan does not have the funding to support the benefit level. When collective bargaining parties wish to direct benefit levels, it is recommended the contract language in the collective bargaining agreement provide a caveat such as "The pension benefit shall be raised to $60 if it is fiducially prudent for the plan trustees to do so."

In some instances the federal government can impose additional funding requirements and benefit levels. Such is the case with the funding requirements established by the Pension Protection Act of 2006.

2. What if our collection efforts will cause a delinquent employer to go out of business? Isn't maintaining jobs and providing current benefits important?

Trustees have a fiduciary duty to make reasonable, systematic and diligent efforts to collect contributions. If trustees do not collect contributions due, they commit a prohibited transaction by extending a credit or loan to the participating employer (a *party in interest*). A prohibited transaction is a fiduciary breach, and trustees are personally liable for any loss the trust suffers. (See page 5 to review what is meant by a prohibited transaction.)

If the cost of collection will be more than what trustees can recover, trustees may make a compromise in a written settlement agreement. Before making a compromise, however, trustees must pursue reasonable and diligent efforts to collect. Trustees should ask questions such as: What are the company's true economic resources? Does the employer have an alter ego company, and can the corporate veil be pierced? Could the full amount of the debt plus interest be obtained if the settlement permitted payments over a reasonable time period?

Before settling or compromising on a delinquency collection, get advice and guidance from your plan attorney.

3. Is there a recommended number of trustees for a multiemployer plan?

There is no recommended number, but the law does require a multiemployer trust to have an equal number of employer and employee trustees. The number of trustees and how they are appointed is specified in the trust document.

4. Do minutes have to be maintained for all meetings? Who should keep the minutes?

Minutes are the record of the actions that trustees take in performing their fiduciary duties. Minutes should set forth all of the advice, information and alternatives that trustees considered in reaching a decision. This important record should be maintained for every trust meeting and every subcommittee meeting.

Who keeps the minutes is not important as long as the person makes a complete and accurate record. In most multiemployer trusts, the administrator is assigned the duty of recording the minutes, distributing them to the trustees and maintaining the historical file.

5. Trustees delegate responsibility to plan professionals. How can we determine whether a professional is doing a good job?

As explained on page 13, trustees may delegate responsibility to plan professionals by following the procedures in the trust document. Trustees have a duty to monitor the performance of each professional. Several factors that trustees may use to monitor performance include:

- Is the professional providing reports in a timely manner?
- Are the reports complete and thorough?
- Are the reports focused upon the performance of the responsibility assigned or are they self-serving?
- Are the reports consistent with comments and information received from others? For example, does the medical claims payer report that claims are being paid in a timely manner, while participants, union representatives and employer personnel managers complain that claims are not being paid on time?
- Is the professional advisor available to attend trustee meetings?
- Is the professional prepared for his or her presentation at trust meetings, or does it appear the professional did a crash project just before the meeting?
- Is the professional up-to-date and presenting new ideas and concepts, or is he or she always two steps behind? Trustees can obtain valuable information by attending educational conferences and meetings. At these conferences, professionals give presentations on what is new and what has worked for other multiemployer plans. Trustees can gauge the level of service and expertise of professionals by what is learned at educational conferences.

It is important that trustees are clear in their expectations of professional advisors. Communication is a two-way street. Without clear expectations and communication, it is very difficult to monitor performance. Many multiemployer trusts have written contracts with professional advisors that clearly spell out the delegation of responsibility and the trustee expectations.

If you are concerned about the performance of a professional advisor, ask for a full explanation of the advisor's responsibilities and activities. If you are not satisfied, consider replacing the professional advisor.

6. Can trustees be paid for attending meetings?
If a trustee is receiving a regular salary or wages from another source, this trustee may not be paid for attending plan meetings. An exception is made for the reimbursement of actual reasonable expenses. For example, Jack, the Local 123 business representative, receives a salary from Local 123. He incurs a $5 parking expense when attending a trust meeting. Jack cannot receive any compensation from the trust assets except reimbursement of the $5 parking fee.

If a trustee is not receiving a regular salary, the trust may reimburse the trustee for the value of wages and benefits while attending the trust meeting. For example, Sally is a widget worker earning $15 per hour whose employer contributes $2 per hour to the pension plan and $4 per hour to the health and welfare plan. She attends a one-day trust meeting and misses one day of work. The trust can reimburse Sally $120 ($15 per hour × eight hours) and credit both her medical and pension benefit eligibility with eight hours of contribution. She cannot be reimbursed for the same lost time and benefit contribution by either the union or her employer. Because lost-time reimbursement is considered income, the trust must comply with all federal and state tax laws when making the reimbursement to Sally.

Reimbursements must be authorized in the trust document. The plan administrator should have a written expense and reimbursement form for trustees to complete and submit with receipts. The completed form and receipts must be maintained by the administrator as a record to justify the payment of trust assets to trustees. The proper payment of trustee expenses is always a part of an IRS or DOL audit.

7. Shouldn't a plan administrator provide new trustees with all the plan documents and the notebook suggested here?
Yes, if he or she is a good administrator. It is the obligation of a new trustee to ask.

CHAPTER 2

Health and Welfare Plans

This chapter provides an overview of how a health and welfare plan is designed, funded and administered. Even if your responsibility is only for a pension plan at this time, it is recommended you read this chapter. Health and welfare issues (e.g., retiree medical coverage) may overlap with your areas of interest and responsibility. In addition, you are probably covered under a multiemployer health and welfare plan. Understanding how a health and welfare plan operates is in your personal best interest. As a result of the Patient Protection and Affordable Care Act (ACA) of 2010, massive changes are occurring with respect to U.S. health plans. Some of the implications of this new law are addressed in this chapter as appropriate.

Trustee Responsibility

As stated in Chapter 1, a plan trustee has a fiduciary duty to prudently manage plan assets in the best interests of participants and their dependents. For a health and welfare plan, this duty involves balancing the interests of the diverse groups that participate in the plan—for example, working members, nonworking members, disabled members, retirees and dependents.

In an ideal world, multiemployer health and welfare plan contributions from employers as well as any payments by plan participants are collected and deposited in a custodian bank. The deposited money would always be sufficient to pay administrative expenses and all the health

What's Happening:
The Patient Protection and Affordable Care Act

For a more thorough examination of the changes occurring as a result of ACA and their effect on multiemployer plans, go to www.ifebp.org/multiemployeraca.pdf. For updates and additional information on all aspects of ACA, visit the International Foundation's ACA Central website at www.ifebp.org/aca.

care needs of each and every person provided benefits.

In the real world, however, the availability of assets to provide benefits is not constant and different groups of participants have distinct needs. There may not be enough funds to cover all the health care needs of every participant. A multiemployer health and welfare plan trustee must make real-world financial decisions.

- Trustees may have to decrease benefits to balance income and expenses. What are the best interests of participants? Which benefits should be reduced? Are participants better served by lowering the level of dental, vision or medical benefits? Perhaps benefit levels should be kept the same for working employees but lowered for retirees?
- If trustees have additional assets, are participants better served by raising the level

of dental benefits for 100% of the participants, or by providing one extra month of coverage for the 25% of participants who are affected by a seasonal layoff each year?

- If retiree medical benefit costs exceed trust income, is it in the best interest of participants to raise contributions or to decrease their benefits to bring costs in line with income?
- How do you balance the needs of one participant who is taking a life-saving specialty prescription drug costing $50,000 annually with the needs of 3,000 participants given a $30 flu shot each year?
- If the new two-year collective bargaining settlement calls for an immediate 75¢ per hour increase in contributions, is it in the best interest of participants to immediately raise benefits or is it more appropriate to forgo benefit increases for six months to build up trust reserves in case there is an economic downturn during the last six months of the contract?

For each of these questions, the ERISA requirement of fiduciary duty does not advise which solutions are best or most prudent. Trustees must obtain reliable information and projections from professional advisors and use this information to make decisions.

Trustees cannot ignore valid information. For example, if medical claims costs have steadily increased at the rate of 10% over several years, trustees cannot assume the increase will be just

6% in the future simply because the lower 6% rate permits retention of the politically desirable current benefit package.

From the discussion thus far, it should also be clear that a trustee cannot make a decision solely on self-interest. For example, a trustee cannot propose a dental benefit increase because the trustee's daughter needs extensive orthodontic care over the next 12 months. The best interest of participants requires trustees to balance the interests of all current and future participants.

Plan Design

The benefit structure of a plan is referred to as the *plan design*. Trustees determine the benefits to be provided and the eligibility rules for plan participants. Both eligibility and benefits must comply with state and federal regulations.

Federal legislation requires multiemployer health and welfare plans to provide each plan participant with a summary plan description (SPD) that tells who may participate in the plan, the rules participants must meet to be eligible for benefits, what benefits are available and how to obtain benefits. The benefits and eligibility requirements must also be included in the summary of benefits and coverage (SBC) document delivered to an employee with enrollment materials or by the first day an employee is eligible to enroll for plan coverage. ACA requires the SBC be formatted so that it is possible for individuals to lay several SBCs side by side to easily compare different plan options.

Eligibility

Plan eligibility may be provided to one or more categories of participants. Some examples are:

- Employees who are covered by a labor agreement and are actively working
- Employees who are covered by a labor agreement; but are not actively working due to an economic downturn, job-related illness or injury, non-job-related illness or injury, or personal leave of absence
- Employees who work for an employer but are not covered by a collective bargaining agreement (e.g., owners, supervisors, office workers)

Tips for New Trustees

✔ *There are some tough decisions you will have to make as a health and welfare plan trustee. Understand the finances of your plan, its eligibility rules, its benefit structure and the role of each professional advisor—including the information and assistance these advisors provide. With this knowledge, you can prudently make fiduciary decisions on behalf of plan participants. Recognize that when you make tough decisions, not everyone will be happy. Your duty is to represent each participant fairly.*

- People who once were active employees but are now retired
- Spouses and other dependents of active employees and retirees
- Dependents of retirees or deceased employees.

Trustees are not required to allow everyone to participate in a plan unless participation is required by law.

- ACA requires employers categorized as "large employers" to offer coverage to all employees who work 30 or more hours per week. In addition, dependent coverage must be offered to children of these employees up to age 26 years.
- Under the Consolidated Omnibus Budget Reconciliation Act (COBRA) of 1985, workers and their families who lose health benefits have the right to choose to continue group health coverage for a limited time. For more details concerning COBRA, see question 3 at the end of this chapter.
- Former spouses are another group that may have a right to continue coverage under federal law.
- Federal law requires some plans to treat certain nonworking employees the same as working employees, such as employees on military leave and employees eligible for leave under the Family and Medical Leave Act.

Trustees may choose whether to allow non-bargaining unit employees (e.g., owners, partners, supervisors and office employees) the right to participate. Trustees may also restrict participation in a plan—A plan might require that a worker have 20 years of industry service to be eligible for retiree medical coverage.

Within limits, trustees can establish how long an employee must work or the time required to meet other requirements before an employee (or an employee's dependent) is eligible for coverage. If plan eligibility is based solely on the lapse of time, ACA restricts the eligibility waiting period to 90 days. A plan may have a longer eligibility period if the eligibility rule is not strictly time-based. This situation may occur when an

employee must achieve a certain number of hours within a specific period (such as working 250 hours in a quarter), obtain a required license, reach journey status or produce a required number of units. This last condition can be illustrated by an auto dealership that requires new salespersons to sell 20 cars to be eligible for participation in its health plan. There is no time limit on selling the 20 cars. Plan eligibility may also be conditioned on completion of a number of hours of service as long as the number of hours does not exceed 1,200.

While ACA generally allows up to a 90-day eligibility waiting period, this time may be reduced if the plan uses a longer period to determine whether an individual has satisfied an "hours worked in a time period" condition. For example, if a plan uses a 12-month period to determine whether an employee averages 25 hours per week, the plan must enroll an eligible employee by the end of the 13th month after employment begins.

Unless restricted by law, rules may be different for each category of plan participants. For example, trustees may require that active employees covered by a collective bargaining agreement work 100 or more hours in a month to be eligible for plan-paid coverage. If the contribution rate is $5 per hour, an employee working under this labor agreement can receive medical coverage worth $900 for $500 (100 hours $\times$ $5 per hour) in contributions. For employees not working under the collective bargaining agreement, however, the employer might be required to pay the full $900 premium amount regardless of the number of hours the person works in a month.

Eligibility rules may limit the length of time a person is eligible for coverage and be coordinated with participant self-payments. For example, an active participant may be limited to one month of plan-paid eligibility for each month that he or she works 100 or more hours. Some plans provide coverage for a full year if the participant works six or more months during a year. If the participant has not worked the required number of hours or months, many plans permit continued eligibility through an hours bank or permit the participant to self-pay a portion of the premium to maintain coverage. In these examples, if a nonworking participant does not have hours bank eligibility, does not make his or her self-payment, or fails to elect COBRA, eligibility ceases until the participant regains eligibility through active employment. The SPD must clearly explain when a participant's eligibility ceases and what a participant must do to reestablish eligibility.

Trustees have the right to change eligibility rules prospectively as long as all participants are notified prior to the change, and the eligibility rules in the SPD are amended. Assume that in January, plan trustees decide to change the eligibility rule on hours worked from 120 to 110 hours per month to be effective in July. This change is for compliance with the ACA requirement to provide coverage to employees working 30 or more hours per week. Federal law requires this amendment be communicated to participants prior to the July 1 effective date—and the SPD must be amended in a timely manner.

Benefits and Benefit Levels

Benefits that are common in a multiemployer health and welfare plan include:

- Doctor's office calls
- Hospital room and board
- Outpatient clinic visits
- Lab, x-ray and diagnostic imaging
- Intensive care
- Emergency room services
- Prenatal and well-baby care
- Surgery and anesthesia
- Prescription drugs
- Treatment for mental illness
- Substance abuse counseling and rehabilitation
- Vision care (exam, frames and lenses)
- Dental care (exam, fillings, extractions, surgery and dentures)
- Hearing benefits (exam and appliance)
- Life and accidental death insurance
- Short-term disability/long-term disability protection
- Home health care
- Skilled nursing care
- Preventive care (physicals, vaccinations, etc.)

- Wellness programs
- Disease management
- Chiropractic treatments.

Unless trustees work in an industry that can maintain a level of employer contributions sufficient to purchase every possible benefit, trustees must decide which benefits will be excluded or limited. Trustees might decide a plan will cover 100% of medical expenses but no dental benefits. Alternatively, trustees might decide to cover 80% of both medical and dental claims. In this second design, the participant has a *coinsurance* obligation of 20%. For a $1,000 medical bill, the plan pays $800 (.80 × $1,000) while the participant pays the remaining $200 (.20 × $1,000). The $200 is the participant's coinsurance. If the participant has a $200 dental bill, the plan pays

$160 (.80 \times \$200)$ while the participant pays $\$40 (.20 \times \$200)$.

Federal laws such as the Mental Health Parity and Addiction Equity Act and ACA have set standards for certain health plans as to what types of care must be provided. For example, ACA requires each state to develop a benchmark plan that details benefits and services for ten "essential health benefits":

- Ambulatory patient services
- Emergency services
- Hospitalization
- Laboratory services
- Prescription drugs
- Mental health and substance abuse disorder services, including behavioral health treatment
- Rehabilitative and habilitative services and devices
- Maternity and newborn care
- Pediatric services including oral and vision care
- Preventive and wellness services and chronic disease.

The states may add other benefits and services as part of the benchmark plan. Qualified health plans that participate in a state's marketplace exchange and insurance carriers providing coverage for the individual and small employer market must follow the benchmark health plan. In contrast, large employers and self-funded health plans do not have to do so.

Beware, however, that ALL plans providing benefits and services from one or more of the essential health benefit categories are prohibited from establishing any annual or lifetime dollar caps (claim limits) on these benefits and services. For example, if a self-funded health plan provides hospital benefits and services, it cannot impose annual or lifetime dollar caps on hospital benefits and services.

Health plans that have not made certain design or cost changes after ACA's adoption date are subject to fewer ACA requirements than those that make such changes. The former plans are referred to as *grandfathered plans* while the latter are *nongrandfathered plans*. For example, ACA establishes limits on the total out-of-pocket

health expenses an individual must pay for "essential health benefits" when a plan does not have "grandfather status." These out-of-pocket expenses include plan deductibles, copays, coinsurance and similar expenses. ACA also requires nongrandfathered plans to provide preventive care benefits at 100% of plan coverage.

Beyond federal mandates and the benchmark plans established by the states, some states have other benefit mandates. For example, a state might require all plans to provide health care for autism or other developmental disabilities. It is essential for trustees to seek the advice of a plan attorney, consultant and medical provider as to how federal and state laws affect plan design, and when federal law preempts state laws.

Even with these government regulations, plan trustees have some plan design flexibility. As an example, trustees might require participants to make a $10 copayment for an office visit with an in-network physician while the copayment is $20 for an office visit with an out-of-network physician. Trustees may also create a tiered prescription drug plan with copays that are less for generic than brand-name medications.

Trustees are also permitted to structure benefits that provide groups of participants with different benefits as long as every participant in each separate group has access to the same benefits. For example, *all* active working participants might be eligible for full coverage on the first visit to a doctor's office, but the same benefit may not start for retirees until the third visit to a doctor. This means a retiree must pay the cost of the first two doctor visits, but an active working participant does not. The key to plan design when providing different benefit levels for participants is to make access neutral and nondiscriminatory by gender, ethnicity and health status. A plan attorney can provide advice on compliance with federal and state nondiscrimination rules.

Experimental procedures and those that are not medically necessary. When designing a plan, trustees are allowed to exclude coverage on particular types of medical care such as procedures that are "experimental" or "not medically necessary." Certain kinds of cosmetic surgery are frequently excluded because they are considered medically unnecessary. Hence, a healthy participant who wants to look like a movie star would not be eligible for cosmetic surgery while plastic surgery on a patient's facial scars due to an automobile accident would be considered medically necessary and be covered by the plan.

Experimental procedures fall into many different categories and can be very emotional. Consider an autologous bone marrow transplant—a controversial experimental procedure for the treatment of breast cancer in the 1990s. Individuals, often supported by public interest groups, filed lawsuits to prevent insurance companies and trust plans from denying payment for the procedure. This transplant procedure was later discredited for the treatment of breast cancer when it was shown that it could do more harm than good for a patient.

As medical technology advances, trustees will be faced with new and different dilemmas concerning what is experimental and what is medically necessary. When a physician estimates there is a one in 100 chance a child has a specific serious medical condition and says a $1,000 medical test will disclose it, is the $1,000 test necessary? If the child is yours, the test is necessary. If the odds are less—say one in 500 or one in 1,000—is the $1,000 test still necessary? What should the "necessary" cutoff point be, and who will make the decision to pay or not pay?

With more specialty drugs becoming available, experimental and medical necessity issues are intensifying. Consider the drug bucindolol, which has been deemed effective for 60% of patients with heart failure and a specific genetic makeup. What about the remaining 40% of patients with a heart condition for whom the drug is ineffective, or the 10% for whom the drug is toxic and makes the patient's condition worse? Will coverage of bucindolol be denied for a heart patient who is the father of three children if the genetic data holds the drug will be ineffective for him? Trustees must consider where the genetic information will come from, who will pay for it and what to do with this information once they have it.

ACA restricts a plan sponsor's ability to uniformly limit what may be considered experimental treatments. The law requires health plans to provide coverage for approved clinical trials that are aimed at preventing, detecting or treating cancer as well as other life-threatening diseases and conditions. A plan also cannot discriminate against an individual for electing to participate in a clinical trial. Further, some preventive services and tests (such as testing for the BRCA gene related to the likelihood of breast cancer) are covered by the preventive services requirement mentioned above.

"Off-brand" use of drugs is a related issue. The U.S. Food and Drug Administration (FDA) has approved Gleevec® only for the treatment of cancer. However, a doctor informs a participant that Gleevec may also be helpful in treating Crohn's disease—a use not approved by FDA. The drug costs $2,000 per month. Should coverage be denied for this "off-brand" use? In another example, a plan participant has Lou Gehrig's disease. The participant reads that Italian doctors have used the drug lithium for the disease even though it is approved only for bipolar disorder treatments. The participant asks his physician to prescribe lithium because it is his last hope for life. The physician prescribes it. Will the trust pay for this prescription?

Minor versus major claims. Plan design requires finding a balance between benefits that reimburse participants for minor medical claims and protecting the participant when there are major medical events. Claims for medical expenses under $500 typically represent 60% to 70% of all claims filed, but only 10% to 15% of total claim dollars. In contrast, the number of claims for medical expenses between $10,000 and $100,000 represent 3% to 5% of all claims filed but 40% to 50% of total claim dollars. Only 1% to 2% of participants have claims over $150,000 representing just one-tenth of 1% of claims—but these same participants account for 10% to 15% of claim dollars.

Another choice faced by trustees is illustrated by Exbitux—a prescription drug that costs $30,000 per year per patient. Should trustees provide participants with full coverage for the small $25 to $50 prescriptions? Or should a $15 or $20 copayment be imposed on all prescriptions in order to provide maximum protection for the one participant who has the $30,000 annual prescription drug claim?

Utilization. Plan design may also be influenced by participant misuse or overutilization of a benefit provided by a plan. For example, trustees might be told that a high percentage of participants are using the more expensive hospital emergency room to obtain treatment for the flu rather than a clinic or doctor's office. A solution to cut down use of the hospital emergency room for nonemergencies is education through the plan's wellness program or a financial incentive to use another less expensive nonemergency care option. In another scenario, a prescription drug provider or consultant might report to trustees that a particular participant is obtaining the same prescription drug from three different physicians, or a specific participant is receiving the same drug from both the state workers' compensation system and the multiemployer plan. Trustees can work with their plan advisors to stop misuse or fraud.

Limits and Exclusions. Most multiemployer plans have cost-containment features. ACA eliminated some of the techniques previously used by plans to contain costs, however. Health plans cannot exclude coverage of an individual's preexisting health conditions. Also, a plan cannot place an annual or lifetime dollar limit on the coverage of benefits that are considered "essential health benefits."

Preauthorization. Preauthorization of nonemergency hospital procedures is a common cost-containment technique. Assume Sally Smith must have gall bladder surgery. Sally's physician contacts the claims payer and obtains preauthorization for the three-day hospitalization that is medically necessary for her surgery. The preauthorization prevents Sally from checking into the hospital a day early or staying a day longer solely because it is more convenient for Sally. Preauthorization contains costs by eliminating hospital care that is not medically necessary. Of course, if there are medical complications associated with Sally's surgery, her physician can obtain authorization for a longer period.

Prevention and Case Management. Other cost-reduction initiatives include wellness programs,[1] tobacco-cessation assistance and dis-

---

1. An example of a wellness program cosponsored by a multiemployer plan is provided in the appendix.

ease management. Plan professionals and medical service provider groups can inform trustees regarding what diseases incur the most claim costs for a plan. National statistics show that heart, respiratory (i.e., asthma), skeletal (i.e, back), cancer and diabetes are the most expensive conditions. Statistics also reveal that 50% to 60% of claim costs are caused by participants' poor lifestyle choices such as smoking, being overweight, alcohol consumption, little or no exercise, diet, etc. Initiating wellness programs to change participants' lifestyle choices is beneficial. Also valuable are disease management programs that advise participants who have a disease how to properly take medication and care for themselves. Trustees must consult with plan advisors on federal and state laws that impose restrictions on wellness programs.

Service Providers

Benefits in a health and welfare plan are obtained through service providers. A *service provider* can be a hospital, pharmacy, physician, dentist, ophthalmologist, chiropractor, psychologist or other licensed practitioner. Trustees may permit participants to select any licensed service provider for benefits (called an *open panel),* or trustees may restrict whom participants use for benefits *(closed panel).* Open and closed panels are options for medical, dental and vision benefits.

Closed-panel restrictions are normally accomplished using one of two methods:

- A *health maintenance organization (HMO),* such as Kaiser, operates a hospital or clinic and employs or contracts with physicians. The HMO typically has an established fixed fee for each medical service.
- A *preferred provider organization (PPO)* is a group of independently employed physicians and/or hospital(s) that forms a business alliance. Each physician and hospital within the PPO group agrees to a fixed fee and service schedule established by the PPO. If the participant goes to an "in-network" provider—one of the service providers that is part of the PPO group—the fees and copays are lower than if the participant goes to a provider who is "out of network."

When trustees select a closed-panel HMO or PPO to provide benefits, the participant must go to a service provider that is part of the HMO or PPO to receive full benefits. Plans typically allow use of a provider with full benefits outside the closed panel only when a participant needs "emergency treatment" inside a geographic area not served by the HMO or PPO. Otherwise, the participant will pay a larger percentage of a higher dollar amount for services outside of the closed panel. The disadvantage of the closed panel is that participants lose the freedom to choose their service providers. The advantage of the closed panel is that the plan and participants have a guaranteed fixed fee and service schedule.

For example, all physicians in a panel charge $120 for an office call.

With an open panel, the participant is free to choose any health care provider, but each provider is free to charge any rate for the service. Normally, a plan pays service providers on a schedule called *usual customary rates (UCR).* If the UCR schedule for an office call is $120 and the physician charges $130, the plan will pay $120 and the participant must pay the remaining $10.

A plan may have a combination of both closed and open panels. A plan might pay the entire fee when a participant selects a closed-panel physician to provide a medical service. If the participant selects a physician outside the closed panel, however, the plan pays only up to the amount in the UCR schedule while the participant is responsible for the remainder. As with an open panel, the participant has the flexibility of choice but the plan is able to control its costs.

Many multiemployer plans separate medical and prescription drug service providers. A pharmacy benefits management (PBM) organization might be used to provide prescription drug service. A PBM has the purchasing power of a large group which increases the ability to control costs. A disadvantage is that PBMs restrict which pharmacies or mail-order services the participants can use. A PBM may assist trust-

Tips for New Trustees

✔ *Meet with your plan's insurance consultant and review the benefit payment schedule. Ask how this schedule is determined and how often it is reviewed.*

✔ *Periodically review costs and fees of service providers and evaluate alternatives. Avoid automatically renewing a contract with a service provider just because that is the way it always has been done. You have a fiduciary duty to manage assets prudently on behalf of participants. You must be knowledgeable of the alternative costs and services that are available in the marketplace.*

ees in developing "tiered" plans that encourage participants to use less expensive generic drugs rather than more expensive brand-name drugs. A PBM can also establish specialty-drug compliance programs to assure that participants taking very expensive drugs are getting the proper dosage and that treatment results are monitored.

Plan Financing

The formula to finance a multiemployer health and welfare plan is very simple: Income must equal or exceed the cost of benefits and administration.

Income

A multiemployer health and welfare plan generally obtains income from these sources:

- Contributions that employers are obligated to make under the terms of a collective bargaining agreement
- If a plan permits participation of *nonunit employees* (persons not covered by the collective bargaining agreement), the contributions that employers must make under the terms of the trust's participation agreement
- Self-payments from nonworking participants such as retirees, out-of-work employees, disabled employees, spouses of deceased employees, and participants continuing coverage under COBRA law or military USERRA. See question 3 at the end of this chapter for a discussion of COBRA.
- Income from investment of plan reserves
- An experience refund from an insurance carrier if the plan is experience rated
- Rebates from a PBM
- Self-payments from active participants.

The trust document and participation agreement establish when payments must be made to a plan. For example, employer payments based on the time an employee has worked in January might have to be paid by the tenth of February. The SPD and SBC may set forth when participants must make self-payments. If a participant wants coverage in March, the SPD might require payment be made to the administrator on or before March 1.

If an employer does not make contributions on time, the employer is delinquent and the trustees have the duty to collect. If a participant does not make a timely self-payment, the participant's coverage can be terminated after the participant is given a grace period (normally 30 days) to make the payment.

Expenses

Employer contributions and employee self-payments are usually deposited into an account at a custodian bank. The funds in the account are used to pay for the following expenses:

- Benefits for the participants (which may come from the premiums paid to an insurance carrier)
- Administration costs of the plan
- Legitimate trustee expenses (see page 6).

Reserves

At the end of the month, if income exceeds expenses, a plan has a surplus that is placed in the trust reserve account. *Restricted reserves* are maintained to pay a plan's known liabilities. *Unrestricted reserves* are normally maintained to provide stability for emergency situations or an economic downturn. For example, if a plan does not have enough income in January to pay January expenses, trustees can withdraw an amount from the unrestricted reserve fund to cover the shortfall.

Trustees must establish a policy on maintaining restricted and unrestricted reserve accounts, and how these reserves will be invested. The prudent amount to retain in health and welfare unrestricted reserves is a balance between the trustees' obligation to act in the best interests of participants for both the short and long terms. Maintaining too high a reserve deprives participants of short-term benefits. Maintaining too low a reserve deprives participants of long-term benefit stability. A trustee must understand the employment and market trends in the industry and the inflation factor for benefit costs to make a knowledgeable decision on reserves. See question 7 later in this chapter for more discussion concerning the level of reserves that a health and welfare plan should maintain. See page 72 for a discussion on how reserves should be invested.

Self- or Fully Insured Funding

The payments collected by a health and welfare plan may be used to directly finance benefits for participants (called *self-insured*) or to provide for coverage of participant claims through an insurance carrier (called *fully insured*). Self-insured is sometimes referred to as *self-funded*. The major difference between a self-insured and a fully insured arrangement is that the self-insured plan bears the risk of claim and administrative costs exceeding the premiums collected. In a fully insured plan, the insurance carrier, not the plan, bears this risk. There are other distinctions between a self-insured and fully insured plan. For example, under ERISA, preemptive state law cannot mandate benefits on a self-insured plan. In addition, a self-insured plan may not have to pay insurance premium taxes to the state. ACA also distinguishes between self-funded and fully funded health plans with some regulations applying to one type of plan and not the other.

Having an insurance carrier assume the risk of loss is only a short-term advantage for a fully insured plan. Once an insurance carrier experiences a loss, the carrier will probably attempt to recover some or all of the loss by negotiating a higher premium rate for the next contract period or by not giving experience refunds in the future.

A self-insured plan can purchase *stop-loss insurance* to minimize the risk of claims costs exceeding income. A plan pays a *stop-loss premium* to an insurance company to assume the risk of claims exceeding an established amount. For example, a stop-loss point might be set for individual claims over $100,000. If a participant undergoes a heart transplant that costs $125,000, the plan pays $100,000 and the stop-loss insurance company pays the remaining $25,000. Stop-loss insurance can also be purchased on the aggregate of all claims. If a plan projects annual claims to be $10 million, it might purchase stop-loss insurance to pay all claims that exceed the annual total of $10 million. In some locales, stop-loss insurance is controlled by state law.

A multiemployer plan may have a combination of fully insured and self-insured arrangements. A plan might fully insure medical benefits

but self-insure dental benefits. A plan attorney and consultant can advise trustees on the advantages and disadvantages of self-insured versus fully insured plans.

The Role of Insurance Professionals

Health and welfare plans depend on two categories of insurance professionals with very different functions.

- **Insurance carrier or underwriter.** An insurance company (e.g., Blue Cross, Prudential and Providence), health maintenance organization (HMO) or a preferred provider organization (PPO) may function as the insurance carrier or underwriter providing medical insurance coverage. Health and welfare plan trustees enter into a contract with the carrier to provide a schedule of benefits for a fixed monthly premium. HMOs and PPOs have dual functions as both insurance carrier and service provider.

  The premium that a plan pays to an insurance carrier is usually a set dollar amount per month per eligible participant regardless of the participant's marital or dependent status (e.g., $900 per month per active participant). However, some insurance contracts break out the premium separately for each employee, spouse and dependent (e.g., participant $250, spouse $250, child $100).

These entities may also serve as the network provider for self-insured plans, giving these plans access to preferred health care providers and discounted services. In these situations, the plan is still responsible for claim costs, and the plan pays the carrier an access or administrative fee.

- **Insurance consultant or broker.** Health and welfare plan trustees receive advice from insurance consultants and brokers on types and levels of benefits, underwriting, plan costs and premium rates. A consultant or broker can be for medical, dental, vision, prescription drug, life or disability insurance. A consultant can provide information on projected costs and income so that trustees can make future funding decisions. For example, if medical claims increase by 10% each year and the current premium is $750, trustees will need $998.25 to fund the same benefit design in three years. Trustees often delegate the responsibility for negotiating the contract with an insurance carrier to an insurance consultant or broker.

The consultant or broker should periodically review and audit health and welfare claims submitted by participants to advise trustees how benefits are being utilized and if claims are being paid in a timely manner. Trustees want to ensure that participants are actually receiving the correct benefits. Trustees also want to avoid billing errors, paying for services not provided, paying for services not in the contract and being double-billed. Often a consultant claims review or claims audit is coordinated with the plan administrator, auditor and insurance carrier.

Claims Payment Procedures

The SPD must inform plan participants what procedures are required to obtain plan benefits and how to file a claim. Normally, the plan or the insurance carrier will issue participants an identification card for the plan. When a participant visits a service provider, the provider asks the participant to show this card and complete a claim form. The provider submits the claim to the insurance carrier or other designated claims payer for payment. If the service provider is an HMO or PPO, the billing procedure is simplified because all the physicians or hospitals are within the same organization.

The SPD must also provide participants with information on how to file an appeal if a claim is denied. From time to time trustees are called on to decide if an appeal should be granted or denied. Many multiemployer trusts appoint a claims appeal committee to make such determinations. More information on claim appeals is located on pages 85 and 86.

Confidentiality and Privacy

HIPAA

The Health Insurance Portability and Accountability Act (HIPAA) established confidentiality and privacy rules for health and welfare plans to protect the health information of plan participants. The purpose of HIPAA is to protect the

---

Tips for New Trustees

✔ *Visit your plan administrator to review your plan's claim and appeal procedures. Keep an updated SPD, a copy of a claim form and a sample plan ID card in your trustee notebook. In the majority of cases, claim denials are due to the employee or dependent not being eligible to participate in the plan, or to inaccurate or incomplete information. For example, a participant complains a medical bill was not paid for his son's injury. Upon investigation, it is found that the participant provided a different Social Security number for his son on the enrollment form compared to the number given on the claim form. This claim appeal can be easily resolved if the participant proves the son is a bona fide dependent and the discrepancy of the Social Security numbers is satisfactorily explained.*

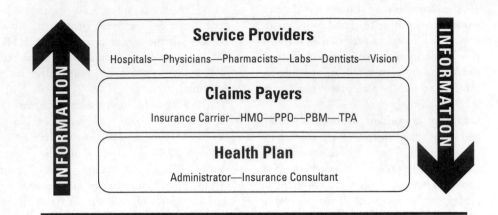

Service Providers

Hospitals—Physicians—Pharmacists—Labs—Dentists—Vision

Claims Payers

Insurance Carrier—HMO—PPO—PBM—TPA

Health Plan

Administrator—Insurance Consultant

INFORMATION

Union   **Employers**

privacy of individuals by keeping unauthorized people from seeing their health information. Exhibit A provides a simple illustration of the information flow addressed by HIPAA privacy rules. These rules apply to trustees, plan administrators, plan professionals and service providers. Violation of HIPAA can result in substantial fines and penalties.

Jim goes to his physician because he is hit in the mouth during a baseball game. The doctor treats Jim's cut, prescribes drugs for pain and to prevent infection, and sends him to the lab for a blood test. Jim also goes to his dentist for treatment of a chipped tooth. The treatment, lab test, dental work and prescription drugs are all *protected health information (PHI)* concerning Jim. All of the service providers involved in the care of Jim have a duty to keep the PHI confidential and must provide Jim with their confidentiality policy.

The physician, lab, pharmacist and dentist send bills for Jim's treatment to an insurance company and other claim payers. The insurance company has information on Jim's eligibility for coverage and the premiums that Jim's multiemployer plan pays for his coverage. The insurance company and the health plan have a duty to keep

confidential Jim's PHI regarding his eligibility and the cost of his treatment. The insurance company and the health plan must also provide Jim with a copy of their HIPAA privacy protection policies.

Note how a bold line separates service providers, claims payers and the health plan from the union and employers in Exhibit A. Those above the line can communicate with each other about Jim's PHI without Jim's permission. This means the lab can provide Jim's doctor with lab test results. The insurance company can ask the physician whether the correct treatment billing code was used. The physician can also contact the health plan regarding Jim's eligibility for coverage. These exchanges of Jim's PHI provide examples of what can be done without written permission from Jim.

Let's now assume that Jim asks his personnel manager or union representative a question about the bill from his doctor or dentist. The union representative assists Jim by contacting the health plan administrator or the insurance carrier about the bill. The health plan administrator and the claims payer are not allowed to release any information to the union representative, the personnel manager or any other person below the bold line in Exhibit A without getting specific written permission from Jim that allows the release of information.

Health plan trustees are bound by the privacy protection policy of their benefit plan as well as HIPAA to keep the PHI of each plan participant confidential. The best practice for trustees is to limit all exposure to PHI. This is done by having the claims payer, administrative service provider and insurance consultants deidentify all health data used by trustees to manage the plan. *Deidentify* is simply a process of removing names, Social Security numbers, addresses, phone numbers and any other data that might identify a specific participant in a report.

Trustees can be given *aggregate health information;* for example:

- Fifteen claims exceeded $150,000 during the plan year—four of these claims were heart conditions, three were premature births, two were severe burns and six were cancer-related.
- The plan has 2,008 active participants, 3,928 dependents and 1,282 retirees.
- Active claims for the year totaled $10.5 million. There was another $14.2 million in dependent claims, $12.6 million in retiree claims, etc.
- The number of participants in each program and the types of conditions being treated.

Trustees do not need to know the identity of each of the participants who received treatment or filed a claim. If a trustee knows the identity of one or more of the participants because the person was an employee of the employer trustee or a member of the union that a trustee represents, the trustee must follow HIPAA privacy rules for that individual's PHI.

Other Regulations

The Genetic Information and Nondiscrimination Act (GINA) of 2008 has confidentiality requirements for an individual's genetic medical information. GINA may also apply to wellness programs that require a participant to complete a health assessment form. The Americans with Disabilities Act (ADA) and the Family and Medical Leave Act (FMLA) have medical confidentiality requirements as well. The ADA and FMLA privacy requirements may apply if a multiemployer plan provides short- and long-term disability benefits.

Common Questions and Answers

1. **Is self-funded a better way to finance a health and welfare plan than fully insured?**
   There is no best or better answer here. Review this question periodically with your plan insurance consultant or broker, administrator and attorney. The stability of an industry, utilization of benefits and tolerance for risk are important considerations. If an industry is unstable and plan reserves are used to smooth out the peaks and valleys of changing economic conditions, a fully insured plan has less risk. On the other hand, if a plan is located in a state that has a substantial number of benefit mandates that apply to fully insured plans and high premium taxes, then self-funding may be more favorable from an economic perspective. Know and understand the pros and cons of each funding alternative with respect to your plan. What is good for a plan in another industry or geographical area may not be good for your plan.

2. **How does an hours bank work?**
   An hours bank can be used by a multiemployer health and welfare plan to smooth out eligibility for participants who work in a cyclical industry. Assume the Construction Workers Health and Welfare Plan requires 120 hours of work per month for eligibility. Mary, a construction worker, averages 180 hours during peak construction months but works zero to 80 hours in low months. An hours bank system deposits hours into a bank in the months Mary works over 120 hours. Mary can withdraw hours from the bank in the months she works less than 120 hours.
   Table 5-I on page 81 illustrates the hours bank concept for Mary, who continues to receive eligibility in October, November and

Table 2-I

Sample Hours Bank

Month	Hours Worked	Hours Needed for Eligibility	Hours in Bank
June	170	120	50
July	190	120	120
August	180	120	180
September	120	120	180
October	110	120	170
November	70	120	120
December	0	120	0

December by withdrawing hours from her hours bank. Some multiemployer plans use a dollar bank instead of an hours bank. For example, all contributions over $500 per month made on behalf of Mary are put in her dollar bank. The principle of the hours bank and dollar bank is the same. A further discussion of an hours bank is on pages 80 and 81.

3. What is COBRA?

COBRA stands for the Consolidated Omnibus Budget Reconciliation Act of 1985. This federal law requires a group medical plan with 20 or more participants to permit participants who lose coverage to continue participation in the plan for a limited period by making self-payments. Loss of coverage for a participant must be due to a qualifying event such as a lack of qualifying hours (e.g., due to termination, retirement, layoff or disability), divorce or legal separation. A dependent's loss of coverage due to the terms of the plan (e.g., exceeding the maximum age, marriage) is also covered under COBRA.

The length of time coverage may be continued under COBRA ranges from 18 to 36 months, depending on the qualifying event. COBRA is very specific as to the eligibility notice that participants must be given, what information regarding COBRA must be in

the SPD, the time limits that a participant has to elect and pay for continuation of medical coverage, and when COBRA coverage ceases. The plan attorney is responsible for keeping trustees advised of any changes in COBRA and how the changes will affect a plan.

4. What should we do if some trustees want to raise the self-payment rate for retiree medical coverage while other trustees are arguing retirees are on fixed incomes and cannot afford an increase?

As discussed previously, trustees have a fiduciary duty to act in the best interests of participants. With limited funds and assets, you must balance the interests of all participants. Consider factors such as the stability of the industry and the long-term interests of retirees.

If your industry employment base is declining and more workers are retiring, a modest increase in retiree self-payments today may

Tips for New Trustees

✔ As a new trustee, meet with your plan administrator to review the plan's COBRA notice and self-payment procedures. Place a copy of the COBRA notice in your trustee notebook.

offset a major decrease in benefits for retirees in the future. The fairness of requiring retirees on a fixed income to pay more must be balanced with the fairness of having other categories of participants (e.g., active working employees, disabled employees, employees out of work) subsidize retirees.

Also explore alternatives. To save costs and maintain benefits, is there a PPO or HMO the plan can make available to retirees as an alternative? Obtain as much information as possible on projected income and expenses. Having good information and understanding the alternatives will help you make a prudent decision on behalf of all participants, including retirees.

It is helpful to maintain good communication with all participants, especially retirees. Retirees tend to believe that once they leave work, they are abandoned and unwanted. Trustees can communicate to retirees that they care. If retirees are given information on why a decision was made, they may not agree with the result, but they will know you made a well-reasoned decision with their long-term interests in mind.

5. **Must health and welfare benefits be provided to employees when their employer is delinquent on payments?**
The SPD should specifically address this issue and inform participants what will occur if their employer is delinquent. Your plan attorney should assist you in drafting the appropriate language for the SPD and a delinquency collection procedure.

Under ERISA at this time, trustees are required only to provide participants with COBRA when an employer is delinquent. Trustees do, however, have a duty to pursue the delinquency and collect. Once delinquent contributions are collected, the benefits for eligible participants can be reinstated retroactively and the COBRA premiums returned to the participant. In addition, ACA permits an employee to obtain health coverage from a marketplace exchange if the employer is delinquent in contributions to the multiemployer health plan.

6. **If a health and welfare plan is in financial trouble, can money from an overfunded pension plan be transferred to the plan that is in trouble?**
No. Trustees of a pension fund have a fiduciary duty to participants to use the assets of the fund to provide pension benefits. A transfer of assets from a pension plan to a health and welfare plan is a breach of fiduciary duty. However, there may be an alternative solution. If the pension fund is actuarially overfunded, and the actuary informs pension trustees that current contributions are not necessary to meet funding obligations, the collective bargaining parties could meet and agree to a revision to the collective bargaining agreement that changes the level of contributions required for the two funds. Let's say the pension contribution is $3 per hour, but the actuary reports only $2 is necessary for pension plan funding. The collective bargaining parties could agree to amend the current labor agreement and decrease the pension contribution by $1 per hour and increase the health and welfare contribution by $1 per hour. This alternative needs the full cooperation of the collective bargaining parties and the trustees of both funds. It should not be undertaken without the competent advice and assistance of legal counsel.

7. **How much should our health and welfare plan have in reserves?**
A multiemployer plan normally has two types of reserves: restricted and unrestricted. *Restricted reserves* are to meet all of the legal obligations if the plan terminates. These obligations include premiums to the insurance carrier, administrative expenses and, if self-insured, a reserve for incurred but not reported (IBNR) claims. An *IBNR claim* is a claim that a participant incurs during a month of eligibility but does not report until several months later (e.g., going to the doctor in January but not submitting a claim for the doctor's bill until April). Always maintain an amount in the restricted reserve that the administrator,

attorney, accountant and insurance consultant advise is prudent and necessary to meet all legal obligations.

Unrestricted reserves are funds in addition to the amount necessary to meet legal obligations if the plan terminates. The amount of unrestricted reserves depends on trustee policy. These reserves can help a trust maintain benefit stability over the long term. If a trust has several months of income that exceed costs, you can increase the amount in the unrestricted reserves for use when there is an economic downturn and income does not meet costs. The alternative to having unrestricted reserves is increasing benefits in good times and decreasing benefits in lean times; this approach does not provide stability for participants.

Study the financial history of your trust, the trends in industry collective bargaining and the future economic outlook of the industry. If the collective bargaining history of the industry is a large contribution increase at the beginning of a contract term with little or no increase at the end of the term, it may be wise to build reserves during the first six months of a new labor contract to provide stability during the last six months. If the industry is cyclical, it may be wise to build reserves during months of high employment to offset months of low employment. Each multiemployer plan is unique and faces different financial challenges. Your plan administrator, accountant and consultant can advise you on the level of reserves necessary to help maintain benefit stability over the long term.

Both restricted and unrestricted reserve funds must be invested wisely and prudently (see Chapter 4).

CHAPTER 3

Pension Plans

Even if you are serving only as a trustee of a health and welfare plan, it is recommended that you read this chapter. Pension issues (e.g., retiree medical coverage) may overlap into a health and welfare plan trustee's areas of interest and responsibilities.

The purpose of this chapter is to give you an overview of the design, funding and administration of multiemployer pension plans. Sometimes, multiemployer pension plans are referred to as retirement plans, annuity plans or another term that means providing income to a participant at retirement. In addition to providing retirement benefits, trustees may want to use a pension plan to provide income protection to participants who become disabled before reaching retirement age. The cost of providing a disability benefit to a small number of participants affects the level of retirement benefits that can be provided to the majority of participants who reach normal retirement age.

Trustee Responsibility

Trustees of a multiemployer pension plan have a fiduciary duty to manage the assets of the plan in the best interest of participants. New trustees quickly discover that a pension plan cannot be all things to all people; some benefits favor one group of participants over another group. The diverse needs and interests of all participants must be balanced.

Pension policy and objectives guide trustees in managing plan assets. Professional advisors can assist plan trustees in defining these policies and objectives. While the objective of one pension plan might be to provide each member who has 25 years of service a pension benefit that equals 60% of a member's final working wage at the age of 65, another plan's objective might be to provide each member who has 30 years of service a pension benefit that equals 80% of the member's final working income by combining the plan's pension benefit with the benefit the member will receive from Social Security.

Assume your pension plan's current benefit is $40 per unit of credit. A participant who retires with 25 units of credit will receive a pension annuity of $1,000 per month ($40 × 25 units of credit). Further assume the average industry wage is $15 per hour and the average participant works 1,800 hours per year for a $27,000 ($15 × 1,800 hours) annual gross income. A $1,000 per month pension benefit is equal to $12,000 per year, or 45% of the worker's current $27,000 annual gross income. If 45% of the average industry wage is the trustees' benefit objective, how will trustees continue to meet this 45% benefit objective five, ten, 15 and 20 years from now? If wages increase at 4% per year, the plan's current $40 benefit must be $48 in five years and $56 in ten years to continue the 45% objective. How will this goal be financed?

A new trustee should understand the basic principles of how a pension plan works, what it costs to provide different pension benefits (e.g., early, disability and normal retirement) and how each of these benefits interacts with the plan as a whole. Benefit changes and adjustments are a political reality of the collective bargaining process, and federal law may mandate some benefit changes. Keeping abreast of these changes is essential.

Tips for New Trustees

✔ *Manage your pension plan for the long term. Pension contributions made today will provide retirement benefits for participants in the future. Understand both the benefit objectives and the investment policy established for your plan.*

Categories of Plan Participants

Participants in a multiemployer pension plan are made up of several groups. In a typical plan, these groups are:

- **Active participants.** Persons who currently work and whose employers are submitting contributions to the plan on their behalf. Actives are normally subdivided into two groups: vested and nonvested. The *vested* group has worked sufficient time to meet the plan's minimum vesting requirements and has nonforfeitable rights to pension benefits. The *nonvested* group has not yet met the plan's vesting requirements.
- **Terminated vested participants.** Previously active participants who have worked sufficient time to meet the minimum vesting requirements. At present, these participants are not active employees and no contributions are being made on their behalf. Vested participants do not forfeit their vested benefit rights. When they meet a plan's requirements for retirement, they

may apply for and draw benefits. See page 45 for more information on accumulating vesting credits.

- **Terminated nonvested participants.** Previously active participants who have not worked sufficient time to meet the minimum vesting requirements. If a terminated nonvested participant does not return to the plan as an active participant within a specified number of years as defined in plan documents, the person forfeits his or her rights to benefits under the plan. Once a person forfeits pension rights, the person starts as a new participant if he or she later returns to active status.

  As an example, assume a woodworkers' pension plan has a five-year forfeiture rule. Dave participates in the plan for one year then leaves the industry to work as a bricklayer. After 12 years as a bricklayer, Dave decides to become a woodworker again. Dave has forfeited his one year of service in the woodworkers' plan and must start anew. If he had returned to active status as a woodworker before the expiration of the five-year forfeiture period, he would have been able to continue earning vesting and pension credits. He would also have been allowed to retain his previous one year of credits and start earning benefit and vesting credits for the second year. His "break in service" while working as a bricklayer would have been erased.
- **Retirees.** People who currently receive plan benefits. Retirees are often referred to as "in-pay status" by the plan actuary, attorney and administrator.
- **Surviving spouses.** The spouses of deceased retirees as well as the spouses of vested participants who died before reaching retirement age. ERISA and the Retirement Equity Act (REA) require pension plans to provide a benefit to a surviving spouse unless both the participant and spouse previously signed a written notarized waiver of the spouse's right. This waiver is often identified as the *spousal consent form*.
- **Divorced spouses.** Former marital part-

ners who have obtained a *qualified domestic relations order (QDRO)* from a divorce court granting them a right to a portion of a participant's pension benefit in a divorce proceeding. The QDRO is served on the plan administrator. Assume the QDRO says the divorced spouse is entitled to 50% of the participant's pension rights earned between 1995 and 2008. When the participant reaches the minimum age and meets any other eligibility requirements for a pension, the divorced spouse may apply to the plan to exercise his or her rights under the QDRO. The law requires a trust to comply with the QDRO. The plan administrator is normally delegated with the responsibility of properly processing all QDROs.

- **Nonspouse beneficiaries.** Family, friends, etc. of an unmarried vested participant that some plans allow to be designated as a recipient of a death benefit in the event the participant dies before he or she begins receiving pension benefits. A beneficiary can also receive the remainder of a retiree's guaranteed single life annuity. Not all multiemployer pension plans provide a death benefit option; some plans provide it through life insurance in a health and welfare plan.

Defined Benefit Plans

A *defined benefit (DB)* pension plan is one type of multiemployer pension plan. Some multiemployer plans have a defined contribution (DC) plan that supplements a DB plan.

Contributions to a defined benefit plan are pooled to provide benefits for all participants who meet the vesting and eligibility requirements. Once an employer contributes $2 for an hour worked by Sue, the $2 is no longer associated with Sue. A defined benefit pension plan specifies the benefit Sue will receive at retirement. The benefit is normally in the form of an annuity, paid during the lifetime of the participant and spouse. If Sue's plan pays $50 per benefit credit and she has 20 benefit credits, her pension at normal retirement age will be $1,000 ($50 × 20 credits) per month during her lifetime.

The collective bargaining agreement and the trust participation agreement specify the contributions an employer must make on behalf of each employee working in covered employment. Trustees are responsible for managing the contributions and investment earnings to finance participants' future retirement benefits. Contributions must be prudently invested so both the contributions and investment earnings are available to pay the pension benefit promised each participant.

Funding a Defined Benefit Plan

A plan's actuary is responsible for performing the calculations that determine how a DB plan will be funded. Trustees should understand the basic principles of funding a DB pension plan and draw on them when evaluating proposed changes to eligibility rules, benefit levels, contribution levels and investment guidelines. The following very simple example explains the basic principles of funding a DB plan. Vesting and other plan rules are not part of this example.

Assume trustees have established a pension plan objective to pay a $10 lump-sum benefit to participants who have ten years of service. Disregarding investment income, the trustees could fund Jane's $10 lump-sum pension benefit several ways:

- Deposit $10 during Jane's first year of employment to be sure the $10 benefit can be paid at the end of year ten. The problem with this method is that while Jane's pension is fully funded, she may not work the full ten years to earn it.
- Ignore the first nine years of Jane's employment and deposit the $10 in the tenth year. The problem with this method is the risk of owing Jane a $10 pension but not being able to collect the $10 from the employer in the tenth year of employment.
- Deposit $1 during each year of Jane's ten years of employment.

The typical multiemployer defined benefit pension plan receives employer contributions periodically, and the plan earns investment income on these contributions. Table 3-I shows how variable contribution amounts made at the beginning of each year for ten years with 7% compounded investment earnings will yield a $10 lump-sum benefit for Jane.

The first year contribution is only $.59 because the $.59 contribution has ten years to earn 7% compounded investment earnings. The $.59 contribution plus $.41 investment earnings equal the $1 necessary to fund Jane's pension. In year ten, however, the contribution must be $.93 because there is only one year of 7% investment earnings to obtain the necessary $1. The $.93 contribution plus $.07 investment earnings equal the $1.

A multiemployer pension plan normally requires an employer to make a regular fixed contribution rather than a variable contribution. In Table 3-II, the actuary has calculated the trust fund can achieve its $10 lump-sum pension for Jane by having Jane's employer make an annual contribution of $.68 combined with an investment return of 7%.

The actuarial funding principles shown in Tables 3-I and 3-II can be taken another step to illustrate how a defined benefit pension plan is funded. Let's assume Jane will live exactly ten years after retirement, and the trustees want to pay the $10 benefit to Jane as an annuity of $1 each year, rather than as a lump sum. Now, the trustees have a total of 20 years (ten years working and ten years of retirement) to fund Jane's $10 pension benefit. This scenario introduces new actuarial principles into the equation:

- A ten-year contribution factor
- A 7% investment factor
- An annuity payment of $1 per year
- A ten-year mortality factor (Jane will live ten years after retirement).

Table 3-III shows how the trustees are relying on 20 years of investment income but only ten years of contributions to pay Jane's ten-year retirement pension. By averaging contributions over ten years and 7% compounded investment earnings over 20 years, the trust can fund Jane's $1 per year for a ten-year annuity benefit with an average employer contribution of $.51 per year. This is substantially less than the $.68 necessary for the $10 lump-sum pension shown in Table 3-II.

A new trustee should recognize the importance of investment income in providing a pension for Jane. Nearly one-half of Jane's $1 per year pension annuity illustrated in Table 3-III was funded by investment income. Chapter 4

Table 3-I

Funding Based on Variable Contributions
(Contributions Made at the Beginning of the Year and Interest Income at 7%)

Year	Contribution	Interest Over Ten Years	Account Balance
1	$ .59	$ .41	$ 1.00
2	.61	.39	1.00
3	.64	.36	1.00
4	.67	.33	1.00
5	.71	.29	1.00
6	.75	.25	1.00
7	.78	.22	1.00
8	.83	.17	1.00
9	.88	.12	1.00
10	.93	.07	1.00
Total	10	$7.39	$2.61	$10.00

Table 3-II

Funding Based on Fixed Contributions
(Contributions Made at the Beginning of the Year at 7% Interest)

Year	Contribution	Interest Earned Each Year	Account Balance
1	$ .68	$ .05	$ .73
2	.68	.10	1.51
3	.68	.15	2.34
4	.68	.21	3.23
5	.68	.27	4.18
6	.68	.34	5.20
7	.68	.41	6.29
8	.68	.49	7.46
9	.68	.57	8.71
10	.68	.65	10.04
Total 10	$6.80	$3.24	$10.04

Table 3-III

Funding Base on Averaged Contributions
(Contributions Made at the Beginning of First 10 Years and Interest income of the 7% for 20 Years)

Year	Employer Contribution (Jan.1)	Interest Earned Each Year	Payment During Year (Jan. 1)	Year-End Balance
1	$ 0.51	$ 0.04	$ 0.00	$ 0.55
2	0.51	0.07	0.00	1.13
3	0.51	0.11	0.00	1.75
4	0.51	0.16	0.00	2.42
5	0.51	0.21	0.00	3.14
6	0.51	0.26	0.00	3.91
7	0.51	0.31	0.00	4.73
8	0.51	0.37	0.00	5.61
9	0.51	0.43	0.00	6.55
10	0.51	0.49	0.00	7.55
11	0.00	0.46	1.00	7.01
12	0.00	0.42	1.00	6.43
13	0.00	0.38	1.00	5.81
14	0.00	0.34	1.00	5.15
15	0.00	0.29	1.00	4.44
16	0.00	0.24	1.00	3.68
17	0.00	0.19	1.00	2.87
18	0.00	0.13	1.00	2.00
19	0.00	0.07	1.00	1.07
20	0.00	0.00	1.00	.07
Total	$5.10	$4.97	$10.00	

provides more information on the importance of investments and the trustee's role in establishing investment guidelines.

These very simple examples illustrate the basics of funding a DB plan that has only one participant: Jane. A multiemployer pension plan, however, has many participants. A multiemployer DB plan does not identify contributions or investment earnings by each individual participant. The plan pools contributions and investment earnings to fund the benefit for all participants. The basic funding principles, however, are the same whether the plan is for one or many participants. A plan actuary typically develops the funding for the entire plan by looking at the pieces of funding needed for each participant and then adds up the pieces. The factors the actuary will consider are:

- The age and gender of participants
- The average years of service or number of benefit credits that participants will earn before retiring. The previous example used ten years.
- The total annual income the trust will receive from employer contributions
- The number of nonvested participants who will forfeit their rights under the plan. The forfeited contributions and investment income are kept in the pool and fund benefits for vested participants.
- The age that participants retire
- An estimate of the number of participants who will take disability or early retirement each year. Also, the number of participants who will work beyond normal retirement age.
- The average life span of retirees, known as the *mortality rate*. Ten years was used in the example.
- The average age of participant spouses and how long they will live beyond the retiree
- The contributions the employer will make each year based on the average hours the average participant works. In the example, $.51 per year was used.
- An assumption of the investment earnings. For Jane's plan, 7% was used.
- The annual administration expenses.

The actuary develops statistical data on all of the factors listed above and applies basic actuarial principles of funding. Over time, plan demographics and characteristics change. If retirees in a plan are living longer, the actuary must make a funding adjustment.

Tips for New Trustees

✔ *Ask your plan actuary for a copy of the last actuarial report.*

✔ *Meet with the actuary and review the report.*

- *Ask the actuary to explain how your plan is funded.*

- *Ask whether the actuary has reliable administrative data upon which to base the actuarial assumptions.*

- *Ask if the actuary sees major problems if the assumptions are not met. Ask what trustees can do to minimize these problems or risks.*

To help ensure retirement savings are adequate, ERISA requires actuaries to use assumptions that are "reasonable in the aggregate." The actuary must annually prepare an actuarial report and submit it to pension plan trustees for review. Parts of this report are also part of the Form 5500 filing with the federal government.

Congress established additional protections for DB plans with the passage of the Pension Protection Act of 2006. The most sweeping pension legislation since ERISA, PPA '06 set minimum funding standards for multiemployer and single employer DB plans, and established new rules governing the valuation of plan assets and liabilities. The PPA '06 also requires actuaries to include in the annual actuarial report an assessment of the general financial health of the plan. A plan's zone status may be red (critical), orange (seriously endangered), yellow (endangered) or green (none of the above).

Plans in the *green zone* (1) have a funded percentage of at least 80% at the beginning of the plan year and (2) are projected to have a positive fund balance at the end of the current year as well as the next six months. In contrast, plans are in the *red zone* if they (1) have a funded percentage of less than 60% or (2) are projected either to be unable to pay benefits within five to seven years or to have an accumulated funding deficiency within four to five years.

A pension plan in the red zone must adopt a *rehabilitation plan* that will move the plan out of the red zone status within ten years. The rehabilitation plan must include schedules that show fund assets and liabilities coming into balance through a reduction in benefits, increased contributions or a combination of both. The trustees may cut certain adjustable benefits such as disability benefits (except for current disabled participants), postretirement death benefits, plant closure benefits and 60-month certain benefits. Plan participants must receive a 30-day notice before the benefit cuts become effective.

A trustee rehabilitation plan must be part of the next collective bargaining agreement. If the bargaining parties fail to approve the plan and schedule, they are considered in default, which can result in mandated benefit cuts and contribution increases. The default can also result in a 5% to 10% contribution surcharge.

A plan is certified as in the *yellow zone* if it is not in the red zone and either (1) the ratio of the fund assets to liabilities is below 80% or (2) the plan is projected to have a funding deficiency within seven years. If both of these conditions exist, the plan is in the *orange zone*.

Plans in the yellow and orange zones must create a *funding improvement plan*. A one-third reduction in the unfunded level must be achieved by yellow zone plans within a ten-year period while those in the orange zone must reduce the unfunded level by 20% over 15 years. As with a rehabilitation plan, the funding improvement plan must include schedules of contribution increases, benefit cuts or a combination of both. The plan must be approved by the collective bargaining parties and included in the next collective bargaining agreement. Otherwise, there is a default.

A plan's professional advisors will assist trustees in developing the improvement or rehabilitation plan and the schedules to improve funding in the required period.

Advantages and Disadvantages

A defined benefit pension plan has both advantages and disadvantages. Advantages include:

- **Lifetime benefit.** Throughout a participant's working years, he or she knows what his or her pension benefit will be. This simplifies planning for retirement. For example, if the current pension benefit is $50 per benefit credit and the participant has 20 benefit credits, the participant knows that at normal retirement age he or she will receive an annuity of $1,000 ($50 per credit × 20 credits) per month for life.
- **Lifetime spousal benefit.** If the spouse has retained the *joint and survivor benefit,* the retirement benefit is provided for the lifetime of both the retiree and the retiree's spouse.
- **Design flexibility.** Retirement benefits in a DB plan can be designed to meet specific objectives. Trustees might have an objective to provide benefits to participants who become disabled before retirement age. Trustees could decide to provide a retirement benefit equal to 50% of the average industry wage to participants with 20 years of service.
- **Participant investment risk is minimal.** An individual participant does not have the risk of investment loss, because plan assets are pooled. (Nor does the individual participant benefit from investment gain.) If the plan's benefit is $50 per benefit credit, a participant with 20 credits will receive a retirement benefit of $1,000 per month whether the plan has compound investment earnings of 5% or 10%. If the plan has insufficient investment earnings, the loss must be made up by increased employer contributions.

There are also disadvantages to defined benefit plans:

- **Young workers subsidize older workers.** Because an actuary uses averages to fund a pension plan, older employees are favored over younger employees. Assume normal retirement age is 65. One dollar contributed on behalf of a 55-year-old employee invested at 7% equals $1.97 in ten years. However, $1 contributed for a 20-year-old is worth $21 at 7% earnings over 45 years. Both the older and younger employees, however, are eligible for the *same* fixed benefit (e.g., $50 per credit). Remember, the actuary uses "averages" of *all* employees to establish funding. In addition, all contributions and earnings are pooled. The extra earnings on contributions for younger workers subsidize the limited investment earnings on contributions made for older workers.

- **Benefit is not portable.** A retirement benefit in a DB pension plan is not portable if the employee changes occupations and enters another industry. If Bill leaves the woodworking industry after ten years to enter the bricklayers' industry, Bill's vested benefit rights remain in the woodworkers' DB pension fund. Bill cannot transfer his woodworkers' benefit rights to the bricklayers' pension fund. (Note: There is a *de minimis* rule that permits a defined benefit plan to cash out a terminated vested participant if the actuarial value of the benefit is less than $3,500.)

- **Limits to recognition of skill or time worked.** Every plan participant is treated the same regardless of skill or amount of time worked. If a DB plan offers a unit of credit for 1,500 hours worked, an employee who works 2,500 hours still gets just one benefit credit. When an actuary determines the funding level of the plan, the additional hourly contributions made for the high-hour worker are normally "averaged" with those who work less. (Note: Some multiemployer plans overcome this disadvantage by awarding additional benefit credit for more hours worked or by basing benefit levels on an hours-worked formula. Awarding additional benefit credits, however, requires higher employer contributions to fund the plan.)

- **Withdrawal liability.** There is potential withdrawal liability if an employer decides to no longer participate in a plan. See question 2 on page 51 for additional discussion regarding this issue.

- **Potential for underfunding.** Although the plan bears the risk of a poor investment return, participants can also be affected because future benefit accruals can be reduced. If a plan is *underfunded* (the current market value of the assets is less than the actuarial accrued liability), the Pension Protection Act permits a combination of benefit reductions and increased employer contributions to resolve the underfunding.

- **PBGC premiums.** The trust must pay premiums to the Pension Benefit Guaranty Corporation (PBGC), which is an added administrative expense. PBGC premiums are explained on page 50.

Defined Contribution Plans

Many multiemployer pension trusts offer a *defined contribution (DC)* plan as a supplement to a primary defined benefit plan. A DC pension plan does not guarantee a specific retirement benefit for a retiree. The contributions made on behalf of each employee are placed in an individual account. The investment earnings on contributions are credited to each employee's individual account.

Assume an employer contributes $1 per hour under a collective bargaining agreement. During the year, Mary works 2,000 hours, Pete works 1,000 hours and investment earnings are 10%. After one year, Mary has $2,200 (2,000 hours × $1 per hour plus 10% earnings) in her account while Pete has $1,100 (1,000 hours × $1 per hour plus 10% earnings). When Mary retires, she will receive a lump sum of $2,200 and Pete will receive a lump sum of $1,100. Added to these lump sums are any additional contributions and investment earnings up to the date each employee retires.

The funding principles of a DC plan are very simple: "What you see is what you get." Mary sees $2,200 in her individual account, and $2,200 is her current benefit. There is no need for an actuary. The only funding issue is the payment of administrative expenses. Trustees normally use forfeitures of nonvested terminated participants to cover these costs. If the administrative expenses are greater, each plan participant pays a pro-rata share of the costs from his or her individual account. If forfeitures exceed expenses, the excess money is distributed to participants' accounts on a pro-rata basis.

Advantages and Disadvantages

A defined contribution plan is not the most favorable plan for all participants. Such plans have advantages and disadvantages. On the plus side:

- **Portable benefit.** The benefit is portable. If a participant leaves employment in the industry or union jurisdiction, the individual's DC account can be rolled over into another DC plan or an individual retirement account (IRA) set up by the individual on his or her own.
- **No administrative costs after a rollover.** The trust fund does not have to bear the administrative and management expenses of a vested terminated participant when that participant elects to roll over his or her account to another plan.
- **Shorter vesting options.** Trustees may design a plan with a shorter vesting period because the retirement benefit does not depend on averaging and actuarial funding.
- **No withdrawal liability.** There is no withdrawal liability for employers, and the plan does not have to pay premiums to the PBGC.
- **Loan option or hardship withdrawal.** Since the benefit is like a savings account, the trustees may offer participants the option of borrowing from their individual DC account. There may also be a provision in the plan permitting a withdrawal to pay for education, a home purchase or economic hardship. However, be aware that preretirement withdrawals are strictly controlled by IRS regulations. If a participant violates the regulations, he or she must pay income taxes on the money received and,

in some cases, penalties. If trustees violate the regulations, a plan can lose its tax-exempt status, and trustees may be personally liable for fines, penalties and damages. Participant loans from an account are also very costly to administer.

- **Investment choices.** Trustees can but are not required to offer an option that permits participants to direct how the assets in their individual accounts will be invested. While a younger worker may want to invest in the stock market, an older worker may want an investment with less risk. Keep in mind that the self-direction investment option is also controlled by government regulations and is very costly to administer.

Among the disadvantages of these plans:

- **Younger workers favored.** DC plans favor younger workers over older workers; an older worker does not have as many years to receive the advantage of compounded investment earnings. Remember the previous example with 7% interest. At age 65, $1 in the individual account of a 20-year-old participant will have compounded to $21. In comparison, $1 in a 55-year-old's account will have grown to only $1.97.
- **No lifetime benefit.** There is no definite lifetime annuity benefit that a participant can rely on at retirement. Instead, the participant receives a lump sum of cash that he or she must allocate. The participant can use the lump-sum payment to purchase an annuity from an insurance company, but the purchase price that an insurance company charges for the annuity fluctuates daily based on the national economy and financial markets. This makes it difficult for a participant to make financial plans for retirement.
- **Participant investment risk.** The participant takes the risk of investment gains and losses in his or her individual retirement account. Even with prudent investments, stock and bond markets rise and fall. When investment values decline, the participant takes a loss. If values rise, the participant gets the gain.

Let's say Sheila has $20,000 in her account at the beginning of the year and her investments lose 10% over a 12-month period. Sheila will have only $18,000 in her account at the end of the year. This risk makes financial planning for retirement very challenging for Sheila.

- **Benefits vary.** Not all participants receive the same benefit in a DC plan. Two participants who both worked 30 years in an industry can have substantially different retirement benefits based on the number of hours they worked, when they entered and left the industry, and investment results.
- **Poor management.** Participants may be financially imprudent and squander their individual account—defeating the purpose of establishing a stable retirement benefit. These participants may borrow from their individual accounts prior to retirement and not repay the loans, or upon retirement use the lump sum of cash to purchase expensive items such as a recreational vehicle instead of annuities. Participants who receive a large lump sum of cash are also prey for unscrupulous persons with investment or financial management "deals."
- **Ongoing administrative costs.** A plan will continue to have administrative costs on small vested accounts if the participant does not elect to roll over his or her individual account into another plan.

The Role of the Actuary With Defined Benefit Plans

The actuary is responsible for gathering data and making calculations that determine DB pension plan funding. The actuary works with the pension policy and objectives established by trustees, the contribution level provided in the collective bargaining agreement, the statistical data on participants and the funding standards required by law. An actuary has a legal duty to "use his or her best judgment" in making assumptions and calculations concerning plan funding. Under the law, the actuary must annually submit an actuarial report to trustees. Parts of this report must be included with Form 5500, which is filed each year with the U.S. Department of Labor. Form 5500 is explained in Chapter 5.

A pension plan has a long-term horizon. If Sue is aged 20, plan trustees must manage contributions for 45 years to provide Sue with a pension benefit when she reaches the age of 65. Some actuarial questions about Sue are: What investment income will the contributions earn? How many years will Sue work in the industry? Will Sue become disabled? Will she retire before the age of 65 or continue to work after aged 65? When she retires, how long will she live? Will Sue have a spouse at retirement and, if so, how long will the spouse live?

No one really knows the answers to these questions about Sue as an individual. With many participants in a multiemployer pension plan, however, the actuary can calculate averages among the participant population based on historical data. For example, the actuary might determine the average participant in a plan is 35 years old and works 8.9 years in the industry. In addition, 8% of participants take disability retirement, 64% take early retirement, 21% retire at 65 and 7% work beyond the age of 65. Eighty-two percent of the participants have spouses when they retire. The average retiree lives to the age of 76.9 years, and the average retiree spouse lives to the age of 79.1 years.

The actuary must make assumptions about investment income as well. The actuary cannot predict how stock and bond markets rise and fall daily. With the advice of plan investment managers, however, the actuary can predict what average investment returns can be reasonably expected over a five- or ten-year period.

The following are typical assumptions an actuary makes when determining the funding of a defined benefit pension plan:
- The number of plan participants
- The age and gender of participants
- The marital status of participants
- The expected error on participant and spousal birth dates, and marital status (e.g., the participant fails to notify the plan about a new spouse, or lists his or her birthday incorrectly on the enrollment card)

- The average units of service or credits each participant will earn
- How many participants will not become vested and will forfeit their pension rights
- The number of inactive, nonvested participants who will return to the industry before they forfeit their rights under the plan
- How many participants will take the different forms of retirement (e.g., disability, early and normal)
- The average age of participants at retirement
- The life expectancy *(mortality rate)* of retirees and spouses
- The investment return on assets
- Plan administrative expenses.

Once a year, the actuary uses these assumptions to develop and submit an actuarial valuation for plan trustees. The actuarial valuation is a snapshot look at the plan's funding status—normally on the last day of the plan's fiscal year. The actuary places a value on all of the liabilities owed to participants and compares these liabilities to the market value of trust assets. The actuarial valuation permits trustees to see once a year whether current funding is meeting retirement benefit liabilities and what the plan will have one, five, ten, 20 and 40 years in the future.

Trustees have a responsibility to inform the plan actuary of pension policy and objectives, and to provide other information that will affect actuarial assumptions. If either the labor or the management trustees have information on the foreseeable economics of the industry or projected employment levels, they should share this with the actuary. When an economic downturn is foreseeable and downsizing in an industry labor agreement will be by seniority, the actuary must assume the total amount of employer contributions will decrease. There will also be an increase in the average participant's age and service because a larger proportion of younger workers will be laid off. A serious economic downturn may also lead to an increase in the number of early and disability retirements. All of this information is very important to the actuary and will affect plan funding.

Plan Design

Trustees establish who may participate in a pension plan, plan benefits and how participants apply for benefits. The law, however, sets some standards that trustees must abide by. For example, federal law dictates the benefit and vesting rights of participants who enter military service. The plan attorney has the responsibility to advise trustees of their legal obligations and any new legal developments that affect plan design.

The summary plan description (SPD) must explain the design provisions of a plan as well as how a participant may appeal when a pension benefit is denied.

Eligibility Provisions and Benefit Policy

The following are typical eligibility and benefit provisions in a multiemployer pension plan that are communicated to participants in the SPD:

- **Covered employment.** This is the work in a job that is covered by a collective bargaining agreement. An employer is required to contribute to the trust for all workers in covered employment. Sometimes covered employment is called *unit work,* which refers to the jurisdictional unit of the collective bargaining agreement.
- **Vesting.** A vesting requirement may be specified as a length of time (e.g., years, months or hours) worked or a specific number of credits earned by the participant. Once vested, a person never forfeits his or her right to a pension.

  Let's say a participant can be fully vested in a plan after earning five full vesting credits. The plan might give a vesting credit if the participant works six or more months in covered employment for a participating employer between January 1 and December 31. Another plan might provide a vesting credit if a participant works 1,000 or more hours in covered employment each calendar year. Partial vesting credits might also be granted. In the latter situation, three-fourths of a credit might be given for 750 hours (.75 credit $\times$ 1,000 hours) and half a credit for 500 hours (.5 credit $\times$ 1,000 hours).

Federal law dictates minimum vesting requirements. ERISA requires participants in a multiemployer plan covered by a labor agreement be vested for "normal retirement" if they work 1,000 or more hours each year for five years. A trust may also adopt vesting alternatives that comply with ERISA. If an employee leaves a bargaining unit to work in another capacity for the same employer (e.g., supervisor or office employee), vesting credit must be given for the time the person works for the same employer in the other capacity.

Federal law mandates that plans give vesting credits to certain participants even though they are not working under a labor agreement. The Uniformed Services Employment and Reemployment Rights Act (USERRA) requires pension plans give vesting and benefit credit to participants who are called to active military duty (including reserve duty). Assume Jake, a participant in a bricklayer pension plan, is called to active military duty from January through October. When Jake returns to work in November, the plan must give him vesting and benefit credits for the period of January to October while he was serving in the military.

Because ERISA only mandates a standard for normal retirement, trustees may establish different vesting requirements for early and disability retirements. For example, trustees might require 15 vesting credits for early retirement and five vesting credits for disability retirement.

The plan attorney and actuary are responsible for advising trustees on all laws and regulations that affect vesting.

- **Benefit credit.** In a DB pension plan, a benefit credit requirement specifies the length of time a participant must work to earn a credit. The benefit credit criterion may be the same as or different from the vesting credit. As stated previously, federal law requires a vesting credit be given to participants who work 1,000 or more hours per year. Trustees might give a full benefit credit for the same 1,000 hours. Alternatively, they might require 1,500 hours for a full benefit credit. In this scenario, a participant who works 1,000 hours during one year would receive one full vesting credit and two-thirds of a benefit credit.

A benefit credit does not need to be defined in terms of hours worked. It can be defined in terms of other units such as months or years worked. Trustees might provide that participants working six or more months between January 1 and December 31 earn a full benefit credit. Some federal laws (e.g., USERRA) require benefit credit be given to nonworking employees. The plan attorney will advise trustees regarding these legal requirements.

In a defined benefit plan, the benefit is paid in the form of a lifetime annuity. The participant's accrual of benefit credits determines the amount of the participant's pension annuity at normal retirement. Assume a plan has a pension benefit that is $50 per benefit credit. A participant with 20 benefit credits is entitled to a lifetime annuity of $1,000 ($50 per credit × 20 credits) per month at normal retirement.

A benefit credit in a defined contribution pension plan is the actual dollar amount paid into a participant's individual account for the year.

- **Forfeiture.** A SPD must clearly set forth when nonvested participants forfeit their rights to a pension benefit. Forfeiture normally occurs when an employee has not worked for a participating employer for a specified period of years. Plans frequently have a rule that nonvested participants forfeit all pension rights if they have not received one or more hours of contribution for ten consecutive years.

ERISA dictates some forfeiture rules. For example, a retirement plan must provide that an employee's right to his or her normal retirement benefit is nonforfeitable when the employee reaches a plan's "normal retirement age." Likewise, the death of a participant cannot be treated as a cause for forfeiture. Other laws, such as the Pregnancy Discrimination Act and the Family and Medical Leave Act (FMLA), provide that time away from work for pregnancy and other covered leaves cannot be used to calculate forfeiture. A trust attorney is responsible for keeping trustees advised of all forfeiture laws and regulations.

- **Normal retirement.** Federal law requires that trustees establish a "normal retirement age" when a participant who has met the minimum vesting standards required by law can apply for and receive benefits. It is common for multiemployer plans to select 65 as the normal retirement age. Some plans, however, select another age, such as 62. The plan attorney and actuary can advise trustees of the legal and funding significance of selecting an age other than 65.

Tips for New Trustees

✔ *Meet with your plan administrator to review who can participate in your plan and what the eligibility requirements are. Review the various vesting and benefit credit rules including when benefits are forfeited. Also, review the administrative procedure used to process applications for retirement.*

✔ *Always have a current copy of the plan SPD in your trustee notebook. It is virtually impossible to remember the many types of retirement and benefit options along with the different eligibility rules that determine vesting credit, benefit credit and forfeiture. Whenever there is a question or claim appeal, you will have an easy reference if the SPD is handy.*

✔ *Meet with the plan actuary and review the costs the actuary places on each type of retirement benefit (e.g., normal, early, disability). Also, review the actuarial formula used to reduce benefits for early retirement, and the joint and survivor (J&S) option.*

✔ *Ask your plan actuary to review with you what role forfeitures have in funding your plan.*

- **Early retirement.** This is usually a period before the person is eligible for normal retirement. For example, if a plan's normal retirement age is 65, trustees might establish an early retirement period from ages 55 through 64. Trustees may set higher eligibility standards for early retirement than the law requires for normal retirement. For example, trustees might require participants earn 15 full benefit credits to be eligible for early retirement, whereas federal law requires that participants who have five 1,000-hour years must be vested for normal retirement.

In a DB plan, trustees normally provide that an early retirement benefit is "actuarially reduced" for each month of early retirement prior to "normal retirement age." The actuarial reduction compensates for the additional time the retiree will receive benefits.

For a very simple example of an actuarial reduction for a benefit, assume normal retirement is age 65 and the average retiree dies at age 75. Also assume the pension benefit for normal retirement is $1 per year. The normal retirement benefit in this simple example has a value, ignoring interest earnings, of $10 (ten years × $1 per year equals $10). If the participant takes early retirement at the age of 64, he or she will receive 11 annual payments of 90.9¢ between the ages of 64 and 75. The "actuarial reduction" of 9.1¢ per year permits the retiree to receive the full value of the $10 normal retirement benefit over 11 rather than ten years (11 years × 90.9¢ per year equals $10).

Some multiemployer DB plans provide long-service participants with an additional early retirement benefit by not applying an actuarial reduction. In this scenario, participants with 30 or more years of service might be allowed to retire between the ages of 55 and 65 without an actuarial reduction. When there is no actuarial reduction, the extra benefit amount can be very expensive. As shown in the previous example of an actuarial reduction, a normal retirement benefit is valued at $10. An unreduced early retirement benefit of $1 per year for a long-service employee retiring at age 55 will give this retiree a $20 benefit between the ages of 55 and 75 (20 years × $1 per year equals $20). This additional $10 benefit must be funded by the plan.

- **Disability retirement.** Eligibility for a disability retirement normally requires a participant to suffer a disability that prevents the person from engaging in any gainful employment activity. However, some multiemployer pension plans define *gainful employment* as work in the trade or industry. Many multiemployer trusts require a participant to be eligible for a Social Security disability pension to qualify for the plan's disability benefit.

  Trustees may impose a length-of-service requirement (e.g., five, ten or 15 years of industry service) as part of the eligibility rules for a disability benefit. Normally, trustees do not apply an actuarial reduction to the disability pension benefit even though the disabled participant may receive benefits for a substantial period before reaching normal retirement age. A disability benefit is usually the most costly benefit a DB pension plan provides participants. As a result, trustees normally establish administrative procedures to check periodically on a disabled retiree's disability status. Since the purpose of a disability benefit is to provide income protection, trustees do not want to pay disability benefits to a person who has recovered and is gainfully employed.

- **Joint and survivor (J&S) option.** Federal law requires both DB and DC pension plans to provide a married participant with a pension benefit in a J&S form, unless both the participant and the spouse submit a written notarized waiver of J&S. In a DB pension plan, the J&S benefit pays the married couple a monthly annuity for the lifetime of both the participant and the surviving spouse.

  Some multiemployer plans offer only the 50% J&S required by law. A 50% J&S is a fixed sum for the lifetime of the participant and one-half (50%) of that sum for the lifetime of the surviving spouse. Assume John retires and has a spouse, Jane. The trust pays John a retirement benefit of $1,000 a month until his death. The trust then pays Jane a benefit of $500 (.50 × $1,000) a month until her death. Some plans offer 75% or 100% J&S options. To compensate for the higher amount the surviving spouse receives when the 75% or 100% option is selected, the monthly benefit during the lifetime of the participant and the spouse is lower than for the 50% option.

  Typically, an "actuarial reduction" compensates for the additional payments the plan will make for both the lifetime of the participant and the spouse. If the participant elects early retirement, there is also an actuarial reduction for early retirement.

  An example of the actuarial reduction for a 50% J&S follows. Assume the pension benefit is $1 per year, the "mortality assumption" for a 65-year-old retiree is ten years, and 14 years for the retiree's 62-year-old spouse. Since the value of the normal retirement benefit is based only on the retiree's projected ten-year lifetime, it is worth $10 ($1 per year × ten years), ignoring interest earnings. The plan actuary develops a table to equate the value of the $10 normal retirement benefit over the ten-year lifetime of the 65-year-old participant and 14-year lifetime of the 62-year-old spouse. In this example, a 17¢ per year J&S reduction factor is applied. The participant and spouse will receive 83¢ per year for the ten-year predicted lifetime of the retiree, and the surviving spouse will receive 41.5¢ (.50 × 83¢) for four additional years of the spouse's predicted lifetime. This actuarial reduced payment schedule for the retiree and spouse over 14 years equals the $10 value ($8.30 [10 years × 83¢] plus $1.66 [4 years × 41.5¢]) of the normal retirement benefit.

- **Death benefit.** A death benefit may be payable to the beneficiary of an unmarried vested participant who dies before taking retirement. The participant selects a parent, child, friend or other party to receive the death benefit. Not all multiemployer plans offer a death benefit to nonspouses because it is more like life insurance than a pension benefit.

- **Reciprocity.** Some multiemployer plans enter into agreements with other plans to grant reciprocity for vesting. For example, assume Plan A and Plan B both require five years of service for vesting. In addition, assume Sally participates four years in Plan A and four years in Plan B. Under normal circumstances, Sally is not vested or eligible for benefits in either plan, because she does not have five years of service in either plan. If both pension plans grant reciprocity and count the four years in the other plan, however, Sally is vested in both plans with a total of eight years. Plan A and Plan B pay Sally benefits based only on the four years of service she actually spent in each plan.

Withdrawal Liability

The Multiemployer Pension Plan Amendments Act (MPPAA) mandates liability for an employer that withdraws from a multiemployer defined benefit pension plan with assets less than the plan's vested liability. Each year an actuary calculates the value of the assets and vested liabilities for a DB pension plan. If vested liabilities exceed assets, there is an *unfunded vested liability.* If an employer withdraws from a pension plan in a year that the plan has an unfunded vested liability, the withdrawing employer must pay its pro-rata share of the liability. For example, if the unfunded vested liability is $100 million and the withdrawing employer's pro-rata share is 1%, the employer's withdrawal liability is $1 million (1% of $100 million). The trust document must set forth the formula trustees use to determine a withdrawal employer's liability and method of payment.

Some trustees welcome a withdrawal liability because it functions as a penalty for any employer that withdraws from the pension plan. Other trustees, however, view any actual or potential withdrawal liability as a deterrent that discourages new employers from joining the plan.

✔ *Meet with your plan actuary and review the last actuarial report. Have the actuary explain how vested benefit liability is calculated and how the actuary values the assets.*

✔ *If you have a defined benefit pension plan with an unfunded vested liability, ask the plan actuary if trustees should reduce the liability and how to do so. If there is no liability, ask whether trustees should continue to maintain assets above vested liabilities and how this can be accomplished.*

Consider what happens if an employer withdraws from a pension plan because it has gone out of business or bankrupt. The withdrawing employer has liability, but the trustees cannot collect it because the employer has no assets. All remaining employers in the plan must assume a larger prorated portion of the unfunded liability.

Due to the negative aspects of withdrawal liability, trustees of many multiemployer DB pension plans have adopted a policy of maintaining sufficient assets above the point of unfunded vested liability to avoid the potential of any participating employer having withdrawal liability. For additional discussion concerning withdrawal liability, see question 2 at the end of this chapter.

Key Government Agencies

The Pension Benefit Guaranty Corporation (PBGC)

PBGC is the federal agency charged with guaranteeing the pension benefits of employees who participate in a DB pension plan. If a plan has financial difficulties and is unable to pay retirement benefits to participants, PBGC guarantees payments within specified limits. PBGC obtains a pool of assets to finance this guarantee by charging each DB plan, including multiemployer plans, an annual premium. The premiums are based on the number of participants. Even a well-funded plan with no unfunded liabilities must pay premiums to PBGC.

PBGC also issues regulations that dictate some of the funding rules and standards that an actuary must follow. The plan actuary and attorney will keep trustees advised of PBGC rules and regulations that impose obligations on the pension plan.

The Internal Revenue Service (IRS)

Part of the U.S. Department of the Treasury, the IRS is responsible for administering the requirements of qualified retirement, health and welfare plans provided by employers. Plans meeting these requirements are *qualified plans* and receive favorable tax treatment. Contributions to qualified retirement plans made by an employer are a tax-deductible business expense for the employer. In addition, these contributions—as well as earnings resulting from the investment of these contributions—are not taxable income for the employee until the employee actually receives payment from the plan.

A tax-qualified plan must obtain a tax qualification letter from the IRS. When certain plan amendments are made, the plan attorney must submit the changes to the IRS for approval.

The IRS periodically audits pension plans to be sure they are administered according to law. The IRS reviews the trust document, the SPD, the Form 5500 filings and administrative procedures to be sure the plan is in compliance. The agency might review plan administrative procedures to determine if married retirees receive a J&S pension benefit unless both the participant and spouse filed the proper written, signed and notarized waivers. How a plan applies its vesting and forfeiture rules might also be examined.

The IRS has numerous regulations that a plan attorney must follow when drafting plan language, and an actuary must follow when performing the annual actuarial valuation.

Tips for New Trustees

✔ *Meet with your plan administrator and ask what the annual premium to PBGC is.*

Department of Labor (DOL)

DOL is responsible for enforcing the laws and regulations pertaining to fiduciary duty and the rules on prohibited transactions (see Chapter 1). DOL also has the authority to conduct a plan compliance audit.

Common Questions and Answers

1. Which is better, a defined benefit (DB) or a defined contribution (DC) plan?

   The answer to this question depends on the policy and objectives established by plan trustees. As explained earlier in this chapter, both DB and DC plans have advantages and disadvantages.

   Some multiemployer plans have a DB plan with a supplemental DC plan for participants. For example, under the collective bargaining agreement the pension contribution might be $1.25 per hour. The collective bargaining agreement directs $1 per hour to fund a DB plan and 25¢ to fund a DC plan. In this situation, the plan participants have both a DB annuity benefit and a DC individual account. Plan trustees have fiduciary responsibility for both plans.

   Some multiemployer plans use a plan design that combines features of both a DB and a DC plan by using a formula to calcu-

Table 3-IV

Participant	Hours	Hourly Contribution	Total	Benefit Factor	Monthly Annuity Benefit Credit
Sheila	2,400	$1	$2,400	.025	$60
Bill	1,800	1	1,800	.025	45
Sue	1,200	1	1,200	.025	30

late the retirement benefit. The benefit formula might be .025 multiplied by the total annual contributions to equal the benefit credit each participant earns for that year. Table 3-IV illustrates how a "formula benefit" works.

The benefit formula has characteristics of DC plans in that participants who work more hours receive higher benefits and each participant has an annual accrual. The formula also has a DB plan advantage in that each participant receives a guaranteed annuity benefit. For example, in Table 3-IV, Sheila has earned a guaranteed $60 monthly benefit when she retires.

A plan attorney and actuary can advise you on the many funding alternatives and benefit formulas that can be applied to DB and DC plans. Make sure you fully understand all of the advantages and disadvantages of both types of plans each when establishing a plan's benefit structure and funding.

2. What is a prudent balance between employer withdrawal liability and benefit increases?

Assume an actuary tells you there is a surplus of $10 million in your pension fund. If an employer withdraws in part or completely from the plan, should the $10 million be used for benefits, or to offset actual or potential employer liability? There is no right or wrong answer. The decision depends on pension policy and objectives in conjunction with the economic outlook for your industry.

There are several disadvantages for a plan with employer withdrawal liability. First, withdrawal liability may discourage new employers from joining a multiemployer trust. The new employer envisions a number of competitors going bankrupt, leaving the new employer with the competitors' debt. A multiemployer plan is not a service to the industry if it does not have the confidence of participating employers.

Second, when there is withdrawal liability, less funding is available for current active participants. A portion of the current contribution is being used to fund benefits for vested participants who are no longer working. Trustees have to evaluate the best interests of participants over the long term in determining whether withdrawal liability should be reduced.

Many multiemployer plans with withdrawal liability have adopted a policy to reduce or eliminate unfunded vested liability over time. Plans without withdrawal liability have adopted a policy to maintain a specific level of assets above the amount that would cause withdrawal liability to occur. A plan actuary, together with investment counselors, can assist you in establishing and maintaining these goals.

3. What if we disagree with the assumptions the actuary uses?

ERISA requires an actuary to use his or her best judgment in the assumptions applied to actuarial valuation. In theory, therefore, the actuary has the final call because he or she is responsible for the actuarial assumptions being "reasonable in the aggregate."

The answer to this question depends on what assumption you and the actuary disagree on. For example, if you want to assume 12% interest because it will produce high benefits with low contributions but the actuary feels 7% is prudent, the vote goes to the actuary. It would be imprudent to pursue the high-interest assumption. On the other hand, if you foresee a decline in employment within the industry, the actuary should take your advice regarding employer contribution assumptions, regardless of what past contribution assumption the plan has used.

As another example, the actuary may believe averaging investment returns as permitted by the Pension Protection Act is a sound actuarial method to stabilize interest assumptions. You and the other trustees, however, may prefer to set benefit and funding policy based on the actual market value of plan assets. In this situation, the actuary can give you the advantages and disadvantages of averaging, but you must make the final decision.

An actuary should bow to your desires on items the actuary believes are good actuarial practice when these items conflict with trustee duty to set policy. As a trustee, be prepared to ask the actuary how he or she arrived at the determinations and calculations that make up each actuarial assumption. Often, there is an acceptable range from which to choose. Your input is valuable in deciding what figure to choose within the acceptable range. Record all factors the actuary provides guidance on and that you consider in plan meeting minutes.

4. We want to start a defined contribution (DC) supplement to our defined benefit pension plan. Can the vesting be different for the DC plan?

The simple answer is yes. However, ask your plan attorney to discuss the various laws that affect vesting. You and your fellow trustees must determine what your pension objectives

are. The lower the vesting requirements, the more a DC plan becomes a savings account for short-term employees rather than a retirement plan for long-term employees. Administrative expenses for a DC plan must be paid from the income and earnings of the DC plan assets. Administrative expenses are normally paid from the forfeitures of non-vested terminated participants. The lower the vesting criteria, the fewer forfeitures there will be.

5. Recently some participants have asked us to provide a cash-out option for our defined benefit pension plan. Should we take this step?

The answer depends on your pension objectives. An annuity benefit provides participants with a lifetime guaranteed retirement income. If a participant has a spouse, the J&S benefit also provides income for the surviving spouse. A lump-sum option does not meet these retirement income objectives.

Investigate why participants are asking for a cash-out option. Are younger participants looking for more income to spend? Someone may have told these participants that if they terminate their employment, they can get their hands on their pension money if the plan will cash them out. This is not a valid pension objective and should be rejected by trustees. Be wary—In ten to 15 years the participants who cashed out may be claiming that the union and management sponsor an insufficient pension plan because they now have a low retirement benefit.

6. Should we have a preretirement planning program for our pension plan participants?

Yes. This is a valuable service a plan can provide participants. Encourage both participants and spouses to participate as early as ten years before their retirement date. In addition, communication that emphasizes the importance of saving for retirement should occur throughout the working lives of participants. Retirement is a big financial and psychological adjustment, and planning is essential to success.

Evaluate the preretirement program. The presentation and materials distributed should be purely educational in form and content. Many organizations offer to present a preretirement program for participants at "no cost." These organizations may primarily be seeking a forum to market their products.

CHAPTER 4

Investment Management

Investment of plan assets is a trustee responsibility that is critical to the financial success of multiemployer benefit plans. The effect that investment return has on the value of benefits for plan participants is illustrated in the following two examples.

Pension Example. Mary has worked in the same industry for 25 years. In each of these years, Mary's employer contributed $1 per hour to a multiemployer pension plan for 1,500 hours worked. This means her employer has contributed a total of $37,500 ($1 per hour × 1,500 hours × 25 years) on her behalf. Mary is now 65 years old and wants to retire. Table 4-I shows the current value of the $37,500 and the monthly pension annuity that the plan can provide Mary with different investment returns.

As this example illustrates, over two-thirds of the value of Mary's pension depends on investment returns. A small variation in returns during an employee's career can substantially influence the amount of benefits that a retirement plan can provide.

Health and Welfare Example. Assume the following:
- A health and welfare plan has $25 million in reserve. The average participant works 150 hours per month.
- Trustees project the plan will receive a total of five million hours of contributions per year.
- The vision premium is $7.50 per month per active participant.

An investment return of 5% on the $25 million is $1,250,000 (.05 × $25 million) per year. The $1,250,000 is worth $.25 ($1,250,000 ÷ five million hours) per hour of contribution. The $.25 per hour is worth $37.50 ($.25 per hour × 150 hours) per participant per month. If trustees can increase the return to 7%, the additional

Table 4-I

Monthly Annuity Based on Investment Return

	Investment Return		
	6%	8%	10%
Value of the $37,500 invested for 25 years	$87,235	$118,432	$162,273
Monthly pension annuity benefit[1]	$ 844	$ 1,146	$ 1,571

[1]Based on a single life annuity using standard mortality tables.

2% produces an added $500,000 per year. This equates to a $.10 per hour contribution or $15 per active participant per month.

The additional $15 per active participant per month is equal to twice the cost of a vision premium. The extra $15 could also be used to increase benefits, offset self-payments for non-working employees or retirees, or be retained in the plan reserve to stabilize the benefits during unfavorable economic times. In summary, an additional investment return on health and welfare reserves can provide a variety of enhanced benefits for participants.

Trustee Responsibility

Prudent investment of plan assets is a fiduciary responsibility for plan trustees. ERISA requires trustees to carry out this responsibility with the same skill as a person who is experienced in investing. Because very few multiemployer plan trustees possess the necessary skills and experience in investment management, ERISA permits trustees to delegate this responsibility to a qualified investment manager as long as specific criteria are met. An investment manager can be either an individual or a firm. The criteria are:

- The plan document provides for the delegation of responsibility. See pages 7 and 8 for more information concerning the plan document.
- The investment manager meets the qualification criteria required by ERISA. The plan attorney will advise the trustees on these criteria.
- The investment manager acknowledges that he or she has fiduciary responsibility for investment of the plan assets.
- The trustees prudently select the investment manager (see page 68).
- The trustees monitor the performance of the investment manager (see page 70).

Investment Policy and Guidelines

Trustees must adopt a written investment policy that provides guidance in managing trust assets and direction to the investment manager(s).

When trustees establish an investment policy, they must consider:

- Achieving the investment income necessary to meet the funding goals of the plan
- Protecting trust assets from risk of loss
- Providing for the growth of plan assets.

Not all multiemployer plans have the same purpose or tolerance for risk. A pension plan in a growing industry with a young workforce has different cash flow, liquidity and risk considerations than a plan in a declining industry with an older workforce. In addition, trustees have very different investment objectives for pension plan assets than health and welfare reserves. The ERISA standard to invest prudently, however, is the same for all trustees.

Plan professionals can assist trustees in focusing on a plan's purpose and identifying the acceptable range for risk. Their counsel permits trustees to develop an investment policy and identify the types of investments that fit within the policy. When developing or evaluating an investment policy, consider the following:

☐ What type of plan is it? What is the plan's purpose and what are the benefit objectives?

☐ What risk of loss can the plan tolerate? For example, a health and welfare plan in a cyclical industry that needs liquidity and cash flow has a low risk tolerance. A pension plan in a growing industry with a young workforce has a higher tolerance for risk.

- [ ] How many participants are in the plan?
- [ ] Who are the plan participants? What is the average age, average years of service and expected future growth or decline in the number of participants? Is the workforce stable or is there frequent turnover?
- [ ] What type of industry does the plan serve (e.g., construction, printing, hotel)? What is the economic health, expected future growth and stability of the industry?
- [ ] How do plan assets compare to liabilities?
- [ ] What are the investment objectives and goals for the plan, and what is the time horizon to achieve these goals? Examples of investment goals for a pension plan might be 2% above the consumer price index (CPI), 1.5% above the actuarial assumption, 1% above the Standard & Poor's 500 Index for stocks, 1% above the Merrill Lynch Government/Corporate Index for bonds, etc. Examples of investment goals for a health and welfare plan might be 1% above the Merrill Lynch Short-Term Bond Index, 2% above the Payden & Rygel Two-Year Treasury Note Index, 1% above the CPI, etc.
- [ ] What is the time horizon desired to achieve investment goals (e.g., ten years in a pension plan, or three years in a health and welfare plan)?

Tips for New Trustees

✔ *Review your plan's investment policy.*

✔ *Meet with your plan investment manager and review how he or she perceives the investment guidelines. Does the manager believe the guidelines will achieve the financial objectives of the trust? Does he or she have any recommendations or suggested changes that would be more appropriate for the funding needs of the trust?*

- [ ] What are the plan's cash flow needs and what are the liquidity requirements of the investment instruments? More specifically, what are the monthly cash requirements to pay benefits and expenses? If the plan needs emergency cash, how soon must an investment instrument be converted to cash?
- [ ] What are the actuarial assumptions for a pension plan and reserve requirements for a health and welfare plan?
- [ ] As will be explained later in this chapter, are there any investment quality or other limits that should be imposed upon the investment manager? For example, trustees might limit the amount of stock in the total portfolio to 50%, with no single stock issue making up more than 5% of the total stock portfolio. Another limitation might be that the investment manager holds no more than 10% of the stocks from any single economic sector (e.g., consumer staples, energy or transportation). Maximum investment limits may also be set for real estate, international equities, small capital stocks, mortgages or guaranteed investment contracts. The quality of bonds held in the portfolio might be restricted to Moody's Grade Aaa.
- [ ] Are there any limits to be imposed on or directions given to the investment manager regarding brokerage fees, commissions or trading of securities?
- [ ] Who will vote the proxies for securities owned by the trust?
- [ ] What measurement criteria and time horizons will be used to evaluate the performance of the investment manager(s)? The policy might state that the goal of stock performance is to exceed the S&P 500 Index by 1% over a period of three years. In this example, if the S&P gained 10% over the three previous years, the investment manager must attain 11% or more for the same three-year period to meet the goal. Also, state in the guidelines what will occur if an investment manager does not achieve satisfactory results.

Investment managers should be required to notify trustees before making internal changes, such as altering the investment style or strategy (e.g., from a value to a growth style, from an individual managed portfolio to investments in a commingled fund, or increasing the high-yield (risk) allocation in a bond fund). The investment manager should also notify trustees before changing the person who manages an account.

Common Investment Vehicles in a Multiemployer Plan Portfolio

The mix and composition of holdings among different security classes, such as bonds and common stocks, is referred to as a *portfolio*. Some of the common securities included in a portfolio are listed below.

- **Stocks.** A *stock* is essentially a certificate of ownership (contract) between an issuing corporation and an owner that gives the latter an interest in the management of the corporation, the right to participate in profits and, if the corporation is dissolved, a claim upon the assets remaining after all debts have been paid. When you own a share of stock, you own a part of a business. Investment managers often refer to stocks as equities.

  The price of a stock can rise or fall. Let's say Company X has a stock value of $50. When the firm loses its primary customer, investors predict the company's profit will decline and the price of the stock falls to $30. If, on the other hand, a company announces a new product that investors predict will increase the company's profit, the price of the stock might increase. Many different factors can influence the price of stocks: how a business is managed, changes in consumer demand for the goods and services produced by the business, the general state of the economy, government policies, etc.

  Stocks are categorized in different ways. One of the more important classifications is by market capitalization which refers to the total market value of a company's stock owned by stockholders. *Market capitalization*—sometimes simply called *market cap*—is the size of a company. These are the approximate values of companies in the different cap classifications:

Mega Cap	$50 billion or more
Large Cap	Between $10 billion and $50 billion
Mid Cap	Between $2 billion and $10 billion
Small Cap	Between $500 million and $2 billion
Micro Cap	Less than $500 million.

Mega and large cap stocks are the largest and, typically, more established companies that will probably not grow very quickly. Small and micro cap stocks tend to be younger companies that are more likely to grow rapidly. Mid cap stocks fall somewhere in between these other groups.

Another distinction that is helpful to understand is the difference between international and global stocks. The use of the term *international* indicates a group of stocks may be from anywhere in the world except the investor's home country. Obviously, in the United States, this means the stocks represent ownership of companies outside the U.S. In contrast, *global* indicates stocks are from anywhere in the world, including the investor's home country. This distinction also applies to other investments such as bonds and real estate.

- **Bonds.** A *bond* is a loan with interest issued by a corporation, municipality, government, government agency or other entity. Bonds are issued in round dollar amounts such as $1,000 or $5,000. They bear a specified interest rate and mature on a stated future date. For example, with a $1 million U.S. Treasury note that matures in five years, the federal government borrows and pays annual interest on the $1 million to the bondholder. At the end of five years, the bond is redeemed and the $1 million is returned to the bondholder. The holder of a bond is not an owner of a company or a stockholder; the *bondholder* is a creditor. Short-term bonds issued for five years or less are often called *notes*.

  Investment managers frequently refer to bonds as *fixed income assets;* however, the value of fixed income instruments rises and falls just like stocks. Let's reconsider Company X, which had issued bonds as well as shares of its stock. Prior to losing its biggest customer, Company X bonds were rated Aaa—This rating indicates investors believed there was a very good chance the company would pay its debt as promised. When the company lost its primary customer and its profit dropped, investors became concerned that Company X might not be able to repay the money it had borrowed via bonds and the interest due on these bonds. The rating of the bonds issued by Company X dropped to Baa and there was a decline in their price.

A bond's length of maturity also influences the value of a bond. For example, a pension portfolio purchases a ten-year bond that pays 6% interest. Two months later, ten-year bonds are paying 7%. The 6% bond has lost value because buyers can now purchase bonds that provide a 7% return. If the pension plan wants to sell the bond to someone else, the sale price will have to be less than the value stated on the bond certificate to adjust for the higher interest buyers can now get. The reverse is also true. If two months later ten-year bonds pay only 5%, the 6% bond gains value.

- **Real estate.** Equity ownership in land, buildings and improvements are *real estate investments.* An employee benefit fund can directly or indirectly own real estate through participation in commingled accounts, mutual funds, investment trusts or limited partnerships.
- **Cash equivalents.** Short-term investments held in lieu of cash and readily convertible into cash within a short time span (e.g., certificates of deposit (CDs), commercial paper and Treasury bills) are referred to as *cash-equivalent investments.*
- **Guaranteed investment contracts (GICs).** A *guaranteed investment contract* is a deposit arrangement entered into with an insurance company, wherein the insurance company guarantees both the principal and interest repayments. A GIC is an annuity contract, not a marketable security like a stock or bond. The amount deposited in

a GIC can be a single sum or a stream of money deposited over a specified and limited period of time. Similarly, the deposit plus the guaranteed interest can be repaid in a single sum or by a stream of installment payments. Expenses related to the contract may be charged against the guaranteed interest payments or paid separately by the contract holder.
- **Mortgages.** Investors may buy *mortgages—* called *trust deeds* in some states—that are contracts between a lender (usually a savings and loan association, bank, etc.) and a property owner. Most mortgages are *amortized,* which means fixed monthly payments of principal and interest pay off the debt within a specified term much like you would pay down a home mortgage. Some mortgages are partially insured or guaranteed by a government agency such as the Federal Housing Authority (FHA) or the Veterans Administration (VA)—adding to the protection of the pledged property and the credit of the borrower. Mortgages range from loans placed on single-family homes, individual condominiums and small apartment buildings to high-risk apartments, office buildings, commercial centers and industrial plants.

Key Principles in Investment Management

As just explained, trustees must establish a written investment policy. They may also delegate the investment responsibility to an investment manager if they prudently select the manager and monitor the results. New trustees must become familiar with basic investment terminology and principles to understand plan investment policy and to monitor properly the performance of the investment manager.
- **Time horizon.** For a pension plan, the investment time horizon is long term. The average participant in a pension plan works for many years before receiving his or her first retirement check. If a participant in a pension plan is 38 years old, $1 contributed today will be invested 27 years to produce a pension benefit starting at the age of 65.

The time horizon for a health and welfare plan is typically shorter and in a range of six months to five years. Contributions in the construction industry are usually greater in the summer months when there is more work. During this high-work period, contributions are accumulated in a reserve and used several months later to offset lower contributions in slow winter months. As a result, health and welfare reserves for the construction industry have a very short time horizon. A health and welfare plan also has an *incurred but not reported (IBNR)* claims reserve to pay legal liabilities if the plan terminates. Trustees may be able to invest IBNR reserves using a much longer time horizon than the assets used to offset seasonal employment fluctuations.

- **Return.** *Return* is the money gained or lost on an investment. Return may be interest, an increase in the value of the investment or a decrease in the investment's value. Return is typically calculated for a year.
- **Risk.** All investments have some degree of *risk*—the chance that an investment will not achieve a desired return. U.S. Treasury bills normally have a very small amount of risk. Blue-chip common stocks typically have more risk than T-bills, but not as much as small capital stocks.

  Many factors may result in an investment not achieving a desired return. For example, *market risk* is the chance that an investment's value will decline as the result of economic forces that affect all assets in a market. Another form of risk that is important to understand is *interest rate risk*—the potential for a change in interest rates that will negatively affect the value of an investment. When interest rates rise, the market value of fixed income contracts (e.g., bonds) declines. Similarly, when interest rates decline, the market value of fixed income contracts increases.

  Risk can be evaluated using rating services or indexes. For example, Moody's investment services rates corporate bonds. A bond rated Aaa has less risk of default

than a bond rated Baa. The interest rate return, however, on the Aaa-rated bond is normally less than the interest rate return on the Baa-rated bond. Investment consultants and managers also assess risk compared to the potential reward of securities by using historical data.

At first glance, it might seem that risk is a bad thing. However, it is investment risk that leads to investment return. While there is no guarantee, securities with higher risk have the potential for more gain in the long term. The responsibility of plan trustees and investment advisors is to develop an investment portfolio that minimizes risk while maximizing return.

- **Basis point.** When discussing an investment manager's rate of return or fees charged, the term *basis point* is often used. A manager might tell a trustee, "The investment fee is 30 basis points." The manager might also predict, "By purchasing a corporate bond instead of a government bond, the interest return will be 30 basis points higher." Understanding basis points is fairly simple. One percent is equal to 100 basis points. If a quarterly investment fee is 30 basis points, it is .3%. A "30-basis-point" investment fee on $10 million is $30,000 (.3 × $10 million). Likewise, a 30-basis-point increase in the interest on a $10 million bond is $30,000.
- **Duration.** A determination of risk for a bond is called *duration*. Duration involves a complicated calculation that includes a bond's current value, yield, length of maturity, and any conditions such as call features or payment class. A 1% increase in bond market interest rates changes the value of bonds by the amount of the duration of a bond. Let's say a bond portfolio has a duration of 3.5. If bond interest rates decline 1%, the value of the bond portfolio will increase 3.5%. If bond interest rates increase 1%, the value of the bond portfolio will decrease 3.5%.
- **Asset allocation.** In designing an investment portfolio, trustees select assets according to a plan's time horizon, risk tolerance,

Table 4-II

Sample Portfolio

	Current % Plan Allocation	Alternative Portfolio
Large Cap U.S. Equity	20	20
International Equity	16	16
U.S. Core Fixed Income	24	19
Real Estate (Core)	10	15
Absolute Return	15	15
Private Equity	3	3
Real Return	12	12
Total	100	100
Projected Return	7.23%	7.35%
Risk One-Year Holding	7.65%	7.67%

investment objectives and policy. Allocation typically involves choosing assets from different asset classes (e.g., cash, stocks, corporate bonds, government securities). The assets in each class have different levels of risk and return and may behave differently over time. A 1991 study of portfolio performance showed the percent to which each of the following factors influenced investment return:[1]

Asset allocation	91.5%
Security selection	4.6%
Market timing	1.7%
Other	2.1%

- **Diversification.** The primary method of reducing investment risk is *diversification*—the mixing of a wide variety of assets in a portfolio. Asset allocation as just described is one way a portfolio is diversified. A function of an investment consultant is to advise trustees how best to diversify a portfolio taking into consideration factors such as asset classes, security issuers, maturity dates, geographic regions, etc. Trustees hope the positive performance

of some securities will neutralize the negative performance of others. An example of diversification and the risk/reward relationship is shown in Table 4-II.

- **Volatility.** Change in the value (price) of an asset or investment portfolio is referred to as *volatility*. If a value moves up and down rapidly in a short time frame, volatility is high. If the value almost never changes or changes at a steady pace over time, volatility is low. Higher volatility usually indicates higher risk. The *standard deviation* measures the historical variance in returns on an investment. The higher the standard deviation, the broader the range of price volatility.

As shown in Table 4-III, the assumed

Tips for New Trustees

✔ Meet with your plan investment manager and review how the current diversification of assets in your trust was determined.

✔ Ask if the current diversification meets the future needs of the trust and if the investment manager has any recommendations for achieving trust investment goals.

---

1. Gary P. Brinson, L. Randolph Hood and Gilbert L. Beebower. "Determinants of Portfolio Performance II: An Update." *The Financial Analysts Journal*, 47.3 (1991).

Table 4-III

Assumptions vs. Longest Possible Historical Time Frame[2]

(Longest historical time frame statistics are calculated based on quarterly periodicity.)

Asset Class	Return Assumption	Risk Assumption	Index	Longest Historical Time Frame	Annualized Return	Annualized Risk
Large/Mid Cap U.S. Equity	7.75%	17.75%	S&P 500	Jan. 1926-Sept. 2013 (87.75 years)	9.99%	22.43%
Small Cap U.S. Equity	8.50%	21.25%	Russell 2000	Jan. 1979-Sept. 2013 (34.75 years)	11.90%	21.78%
Broad International Equity	8.65%	20.80%	MSCI ACWI Ex U.S. (Gross)	Jan. 1988-Sept. 2013 (25.75 years)	6.40%	19.26%
U.S. Core Fixed Income	3.50%	5.75%	Barclay's U.S. Aggregate Bond	Jan. 1976-Sept. 2013 (37.75 years)	7.97%	6.48%
Absolute Return	6.75%	9.75%	HFN FOF Multi-Strat (Net)	Jan. 1982-Sept. 2013 (31.75 years)	11.84%	7.45%
Real Estate (Core)	7.00%	12.50%	NCREIF-ODCE (Gross) (AWA)	Jan. 1978-Sept. 2013 (35.75 years)	8.44%	5.53%
Long-Duration Fixed Income	4.25%	12.00%	Barclay's U.S. Govt/Credit: Long Bond	Jan. 1973-Sept. 2013 (40.75 years)	8.66%	10.77%

[2]R.V. Kuhns, Portland, Oregon.

future return on large/mid cap U.S. equities is 7.75% with a standard deviation of 17.75%. An investment consultant would explain that 66% of the time in nine of ten time periods, large/mid cap equity stocks will provide a return of -10% (7.75% − 17.75%) to 25.5% (7.75% + 17.75%). For two standard deviations, the return will be 95% accurate within nine of ten selected periods. For large/mid cap U.S. stocks, two standard deviations is 35.5% (17.75% × 2). Therefore, the return will fall between -27.75% and 43.25% (7.75% plus or minus 35.5%).

- **Market index.** A *market index* tracks the performance of a specific "basket" of assets to represent a particular market. There is an index for almost every conceivable kind of stocks and bonds available both inside and outside the U.S. For example, the Standard & Poor's 500 (S&P 500 Index) tracks the price of 500 mostly large and mid cap stocks on the New York Stock Exchange. Another index, The Russell 2000, tracks 2,000 small cap company stocks in the United States, while the Wilshire 5000 is the price of the total U.S. stock market—more than 6,500 companies traded on a U.S. stock exchange. The EAFE is an index that tracks the value of stocks in Europe/Australasia and the Far East. One of the most well-known bond indices is the Barclay's Aggregate Bond Index, which reflects the value of the total U.S. bond market.

- **Alpha.** *Alpha* is the amount of investment return that an active investment manager attempts to achieve over an index such as the S&P 500. A manager will have an "investment style" that theoretically produces a positive alpha. A firm may claim that its "style" will produce a positive 2% annualized return above the index over a three- to five-year period. If the index produces an annualized 10% return over a three-year period, the manager should produce a 12% return (10% index plus 2% style) for the same three years.

How does an investment manager obtain the additional 2%? The manager takes an additional risk above the risk of the index. Assume 13.36% of the S&P 500 is invested in energy-related stocks and 15.76% in information technology. Based on his or her research, the manager believes energy companies will do better than technology companies over the next year and, therefore, increases the proportion of stock in energy to 16% and reduces the allocation in technology to 13%. If the manager's prediction is correct, the change in allocation will produce a return greater than the S&P 500. Of course, if the prediction is wrong, the portfolio may suffer a loss in comparison to the S&P 500. Another way an investment manager may achieve "alpha" is stock selection or style.

The prediction that energy stocks will do better than technology stocks creates a risk/reward ratio over the S&P 500 Index. This additional risk/reward is the *tracking error*. The investment manager should disclose what the tracking error is for the alpha (the 2% additional return) that he or she is attempting to achieve. For example, if the tracking error is 2.5%, the manager

Table 4-IV

Return %

Sector	2012	2011	2010	2009	2008	2007	2006	2005	2004
Consumer Discretionary	24%	6%	28%	41%	-37%	-14%	17%	-7%	12%
Consumer Staples	11	14	14	15	-15	11	12	1	6
Energy	5	5	21	14	-35	32	22	29	28
Financials	29	-17	12	17	-55	20	16	4	8
Health Care	18	13	3	20	-23	5	6	5	.2
Industrials	15	-1	27	21	-40	10	11	.4	16
Information Technology	15	2	19	62	-43	15	8	.4	2
Materials	15	-10	22	49	-46	20	15	2	11
Telecommunications	18	6	19	9	-30	8	32	-9	16
Utilities	1	20	5	12	-29	16	17	13	20

will produce a 4.5% to -2% return (2% plus or minus the 2.5% tracking error) over a designated period in the attempt to produce the desired amount of alpha.

As shown by the shifting returns in Table 4-IV, sectors are highly volatile. This is why trustees want diversity within the stock portion of a portfolio.

Like active stock managers, active bond managers attempt to provide a positive return (alpha) over an index. A manager can achieve this by taking an additional risk, which is also referred to as the tracking error. For example, the Barclay U.S. Aggregate Bond Index has a mixture of government and corporate bonds issued in the United States. A bond manager may choose to carry a higher proportion of corporate than government bonds than that in the index (or vice versa). The manager might also choose bonds that have a shorter or longer average bond *duration* (time until the bond matures and is repaid) than the bonds in the index. Other options available to the manager include buying some bonds that are lower quality than those in the index or that were issued outside the U.S.

- **Beta.** While the price of some investments follows financial markets, others do the exact opposite. *Beta* is a means to assess what will happen to an individual security (e.g., a stock) as compared to the market for a much larger set of securities. *Beta* is the average change in the value of a security corresponding to a 1% change in the larger market. For example, a beta of 0.5 means the price of a security is only half as volatile as the average security, while a beta of 2.0 means the security is twice as risky. A security with a beta of zero means the security's price is independent of the market.

The higher the beta, the higher an asset's

Correlation Matrix

	Large Cap U.S. Equity	Small/Mid Cap U.S. Equity	Broad International Equity	U.S. Core Fixed Income	Absolute Return	Real Estate (Core)	Long-Duration Fixed Income
Large Cap U.S. Equity	1.00						
Small/Mid Cap U.S. Equity	0.85	1.00					
Broad International Equity	0.66	0.62	1.00				
U.S. Core Fixed Income	0.21	0.14	0.04	1.00			
Absolute Return	0.44	0.56	0.49	0.07	1.00		
Real Estate (Core)	-0.04	-0.06	0.10	-0.16	-0.14	1.00	
Long-Duration Fixed Income	0.22	0.13	0.03	0.99	0.07	-0.16	1.00

risk and the higher the return required. A lower beta means less risk and typically, less return. Whether the beta is positive or negative is also important. A positive beta means the value of the asset generally follows the market. A negative beta indicates the value of the asset is *inversely related* to the market—The value of the asset generally decreases when the value of the market goes up and vice versa.

Beta can also be used to measure the extent to which rates of return for different asset classes move in the same or different directions. If the returns for two asset classes rise or fall at the same time and in the same amount, the two asset classes have a beta correlation of 1.0. However, if the returns for two asset classes move in the exact opposite direction at the same time and in the same amount, the two asset classes have a -1.0 correlation.

The figure shows the correlation for seven different asset classes. If a plan has two investment managers and both have a style that invests solely in large cap U.S. equity (stocks), the correlation will be close to 1.0. When the stock market rises or falls, the large cap U.S. equity managed by each of the two managers will rise or fall very similarly. There is very little diversification and protection from volatility.

The correlation between large cap U.S. equity and core real estate is -0.4. Assume a plan has two different investment managers. One focuses on large cap U.S. equity while the other invests in real estate. There is diversification because when the market rises or falls during the same time, large cap U.S. equity and core real estate returns will not be the same. This provides diversification and protection from volatility.

- **Price/earnings ratio.** When comparing one company to others in the same industry or to the market in general, investment advisors frequently refer to the *price/earnings ratio* or the *P/E ratio*, which is the current share price of a stock divided by its current or estimated future *earnings*

per share (EPS). A high P/E ratio suggests investors expect higher earnings growth in the future compared to companies with a low P/E ratio.

Investment Styles and Returns

Investment managers have different styles when choosing securities for a portfolio. A manager may use any of the following terms to describe their approach to investing.

- **Active manager.** An investment manager who frequently buys and sells securities in an effort to exploit short-term investment trends and get above-average returns.
- **Passive manager.** A manager who tries to match the average return and risk of a market or index by attempting to mirror its makeup. Adjustments are longer term and automatic versus the shorter term approach dependent on personal judgment used in active management.
- **Contrarian manager.** A stock manager who places emphasis on stocks currently out of favor.
- **Core manager.** A manager who uses a relatively passive investment style but also mixes in some analysis more typical of an active manager. The core manager attempts to select investments that mirror the assets comprising the S&P 500 or other market indexes. He or she also uses some fundamental analysis of the company's revenue, profit, debt, asset values, etc. in an effort to outperform the selected index over the long pull. Security turnover is limited, which results in lower transaction costs. The price/earnings ratios are similar to the S&P 500.
- **Growth manager.** A manager who focuses on stocks of more stable companies that deliver returns via stock price increases *(capital appreciation).* Growth stocks have price/earnings ratios in the top 40% of the stock universe.
- **Sector rotator manager.** A common stock manager who invests primarily in industries expected to outperform the stock market as a whole.

- **Value manager.** A common stock manager who focuses on low price/earnings ratios, low book value and current valuation relative to historical levels. The stocks have a price/earnings ratio in the bottom 40% of the stock universe.

Advanced Investment Strategies

In order to generate high returns on investments, some managers use advanced strategies referred to as *hedging*. Common hedge fund strategies include:

- **Long/short equity.** Managers maintain both long and short positions in equity securities. If an investor believes the value of a stock is going to increase, they *go long*—buying the stock with a plan to sell it when the stock's value increases. Investors that believe the price of a stock is going to drop *sell short*—they borrow stock from another investor and sell it. They assume they will be able to buy the stock later for a lower price and return the shares they borrowed.
- **Global macro.** Managers have a broad "top-down" mandate to invest in the most favorable global markets. In truth, these are not really hedged.
- **Relative value.** Arbitrage of pricing inefficiencies in equities, convertible securities, fixed income, etc. In very simple terms, *arbitrage* is buying an asset in one market for immediate sale in another at a better price. The investor is taking advantage of price differences in separate markets. Technology has made it increasingly difficult to find instances where mispricing has occurred.
- **Event driven.** Trading in securities that are involved in mergers and acquisitions, restructurings, bankruptcy, etc.

No particular investment style is an automatic winner or loser. What produces the best return today may produce the lowest return tomorrow.

Key Investment Professionals

Investment Professionals and Their Roles

Very few multiemployer plan trustees have either the knowledge or time to make investment allocation decisions and to monitor the performance of investments. As a result, trustees typically depend on qualified investment consultants and managers.

- **Investment manager.** An *investment manager* manages and invests plan assets according to the objectives and policies of the trust. The investment manager should make at least a quarterly report to trustees on the status of the assets for which he or she is responsible.
- **Investment consultant.** Most multiemployer plans utilize the services of an *investment consultant* (sometimes referred to as an *investment monitor*) to advise and assist trustees in establishing investment policies and objectives, evaluating types of investments (e.g., stocks, bonds and real estate), reviewing asset allocation in terms of risk and reward, and selecting and monitoring the performance of investment managers. An investment consultant can provide objective advice to trustees, because the consultant has neither an investment product to sell nor a stake in performance outcome.

    A consultant will use the standard deviation and correlations for different asset mixes

---

Tips for New Trustees

✔ When managing plan investments, it is your responsibility to use your best judgment based upon the advice of professional managers and your prudent review of the facts. Understand the different types of investments (e.g., stocks, bonds, real estate) and what role each type plays in investment policy. Recognize how diversification of assets can reduce risk without necessarily lowering the potential for gain. An investment consultant and investment manager will help you apply this concept.

✔ Remember that an investment manager or consultant cannot guarantee success. However, the professional guidance provided on the risks and rewards of different investment vehicles over the long term is very valuable.

Table 4-V

Annual Asset Class Performance[1]

Style	Annual Return %								
	2012	2011	2010	2009	2008	2007	2006	2005	2004
Three-Month Treasury Bills	0	0	0	0	2	5	5	3	1
S&P 500 Large Cap	16	2	15	26	-37	5	16	5	11
Russell 2000 U.S. Small Cap	16	-4	27	27	-34	-2	18	5	18
Barclays U.S.[2] Bonds Aggregate	4	8	7	6	5	7	4	2	4
Barclays U.S. Treasuries	7	14	6	11	14	12	.4	3	8
Barclays Corporate High-Yield Bonds	16	5	15	58	-26	40	33	34	11
MSCI EAFE (Europe, Australasia and Far East) Large Stock International	18	-12	8	32	-26	12	27	14	14
MSCI EAFE (Europe, Australasia and Far East) International Small Caps	20	16	22	17	17	2	20	27	31
NCREIF (National Councilof Real Estate Fiduciaries) Real Estate	11	16	16	-30	-10	16	17	20	21
HFN FOF (Fund of Funds)	5	-6	5	10	-19	10	10	7	7

1. R.V. Kuhns. Portland Oregon.
2. Barclays was formerly Lehman Brothers.

to calculate the likelihood of meeting an investment objective over a specific period. For a specific mix of stocks and bonds, the consultant might report that receiving a return of 8% over five years will be 20% and the likelihood of having a return of less than 3% for the same period is 16%.

When monitoring an investment manager's performance, the function of the investment consultant is to inform trustees what happened over a time. The consultant presents trustees with both the good and bad news, and provides an analysis. The consultant compares the manager's performance to the proper index and investment style. Table 4-V provides some examples of indices that might be used and their performance in recent years. The consultant normally has access to investment performance data from many other managers who invest assets for multiemployer funds and institutions. This data shows trustees how their fund investment performance compares with other funds across the United States.

- **Custodian bank.** Most multiemployer plans utilize a custodian bank to receive employer contributions and deposit the money into a plan checking account for payment of benefits and plan expenses. When a plan has excess contributions, the custodian bank allocates these contributions to the investment manager(s) according to plan investment policy. When expenses exceed contributions, the custodian bank must receive investment income from the investment manager(s) to meet plan financial obligations. The custodian bank must hold all plan assets in interest-bearing accounts. The custodian bank may also hold trust securities

and make the electronic deliveries for trades as directed by the investment manager.

Sometimes, a bank receives the interest and dividend payments on stocks and bonds. Let's say a bank has custody of 10,000 shares of Big Oil Ltd. stocks purchased by a trust at $18 per share. The investment manager sells these shares for $20 each and purchases 10,000 shares of Good Health Hospitals Inc. for $19 per share. The custodian bank delivers 10,000 Big Oil Ltd. share certificates to the buyer and collects the $200,000 sale price. The bank then transfers $190,000 to the seller of Good Health Hospitals, obtains the stock certificates and credits $10,000 to the investment manager's cash account.

A custodian bank normally submits a monthly or quarterly report to trustees. The report lists the securities in the trust portfolio, the book and market value of the securities, the buy/sell transactions, and the interest and dividend payments received.

- **Auditor.** The auditor issues an independent opinion on the plan's financial statements. See Chapter 6 for a complete discussion of a trust auditor's role.

Tips for New Trustees

✔ See Chapter 7 for a discussion on meeting with investment plan professionals.

✔ Request a copy of the most recent report showing the types of assets in your plan portfolio and their values. Either the investment manager, custodian bank or both should provide trustees with this report on a monthly or quarterly basis. The report should also show the trades (purchases and sales) of securities, and the dividends and interest received. Review these reports and stay familiar with the activity of the investment manager.

✔ When an investment manager changes the plan portfolio asset mix (e.g., shifting market sectors, switching between government and corporate bonds, or adjusting the amount of cash held) ask for a clear explanation why.

Selecting an Investment Manager

Prior to selecting an investment manager, trustees with the assistance of an investment consultant should analyze the investment process of a potential manager. Are there objective reasons to believe the manager's strategy or product will achieve what is promised? For example, an investment firm has an enhanced S&P Index fund. The firm matches 75% of its product to the S&P Index, but underweights or overweights the other 25% of stocks in the S&P Index. Does this fit with the risk and return the trustees want for the plan?

If plan trustees and the investment consultant like the manager's process, examine the manager's historical performance next. Have the manager's returns been the result of his or her investment approach or perhaps just good luck? If the stock market's past three years favored growth stock managers over value stock managers, a growth stock manager will probably have a better three-year past performance history than a value stock manager.

When choosing an investment manager, consider:

- [ ] Is the manager registered with the Securities and Exchange Commission (SEC)?
- [ ] Is the manager an individual, a partnership or a firm? Is the business a branch of a giant conglomerate, or the only activity of a firm? Who owns the firm? Is it owned by outside stockholders or managing partners?
- [ ] How large is the firm? How much capital does the firm manage? Will plan assets be managed individually or be part of a pooled account? Will the account to be managed be a major or minor part of the firm's business? How much individual attention will be given to the account?
- [ ] Does the management firm have any internal guidelines on the maximum percent of a portfolio that can be invested in a single sector or security? What capitalization parameters, return objectives, buy/sell disciplines or portfolio characteristics will be used? Does this meet with your plan's purpose and objectives, and trustee sensitivity to risk?
- [ ] Who will be in charge of the account? Who will actually make the asset allocation and buy/sell decisions? What are his or her credentials? What backup in terms of research, analysis, marketing, administration, etc., is provided by the manager's firm?
- [ ] What is the manager's style and philosophy?
- [ ] What is the manager's experience with the type of investments (e.g., stocks, bonds and real estate) to be managed?
- [ ] What is the investment objective of the other accounts for which the manager is responsible? For example, the other four accounts are high-risk stock growth accounts, and yours is a low-risk pension plan in a declining industry.
- [ ] What is the maximum number of accounts an individual manager is permitted to handle? How many other accounts will the person assigned to manage the plan account have? Will your fund be a major or minor part of his or her account responsibility? For example, if the manager has four $50 million accounts and yours is $5 million, will your $5 million account get the same attention and be as important as the four $50 million accounts?
- [ ] What is the availability of the manager to give reports to trustees and attend trustee meetings? What kind and type of reports does the manager give?
- [ ] What is the manager's performance record for the past year, three years and five years for the type(s) of investment to be managed? Many times an investment management firm gives performance figures based on the firm's average versus individual manager's. Is the performance of the person(s) who will handle the account below, at or above the firm average?
- [ ] Is the performance figure that the manager quotes net or gross in relation to fees paid to the manager? If the manager charges a 50-basis-point fee and the advertised investment return is 8%, is the 8% "net of fees"? If not, the actual return is 7½%.
- [ ] What experience have other multiemployer plans with objectives similar to your plan had with this manager? The prospective manager should provide references for both current and former multiemployer accounts.
- [ ] What reputation does the manager and firm have with other plan professionals who advise the plan? Keep in mind that some plan professionals are likely employed by firms performing services for other plans. A plan's professional advisor can poll firms that may have had experiences with a potential candidate.
- [ ] How many accounts has the manager obtained and lost during the past two years? Why did the manager lose the accounts? Talk to persons affiliated with trust funds that have stopped doing business with the manager, as well as the manager's current clients. Ask for their opinions regarding their experience with the manager.
- [ ] Does the manager have errors and omissions insurance, fidelity bonding and fiduciary liability insurance? If so, how much?
- [ ] What are the manager's fees, and how do they compare with others who perform the

same service(s)? Are the fees fixed or negotiable? Trustees are not always obligated to choose the firm with the lowest fee, however, trustees are obligated to justify why participants will benefit from a selected firm with a higher fee. The justification might include a history of producing a higher return, a more stable firm, more expertise in the investment area, etc.

Before selecting an investment manager, obtain answers to the considerations outlined above and compare the answers for several managers. Also, ask other plan professionals for advice and assistance.

Paying an Investment Manager

Investment managers charge a fee in exchange for their services. This fee is normally paid on a quarterly basis and equals a percentage (basis points) of the total market value of the assets under management. Let's say the quarterly management fee is 50 basis points and the market value of the portfolio is $10 million; in this case, the fee would be $50,000 (.5 × $10 million).

A management fee can be a variable or flat amount. A flat fee might be 30 basis points on $100 million. The fee may also be determined by a formula, such as 50 basis points on the first $10 million, 35 basis points on the next $40 million and 20 basis points on all assets over $50 million. Many investment managers charge a higher fee schedule for managing specialty investments such as small capital stock, foreign market investments, real estate, etc.

It is important to understand what the management fee covers. Does the fee cover the invest-

ment manager attending trustee meetings and giving reports? Is the manager giving plan investments individual attention, or are assets mixed in a pooled account with those of other plans? The management fee should be lower when the manager uses a pooled or mutual fund rather than managing plan assets as an individual account.

In many instances services and fees are negotiable. An investment consultant can advise trustees when investment management prices are too high and when to negotiate. The investment consultant can also provide a warning "when a deal sounds too good to be true. . . ." The investment consultant has the data and information on fees and performance comparisons of hundreds of investment managers across the United States.

Monitoring the Performance of an Investment Manager

Monitoring performance requires a measurement system be defined in the plan investment policy. Trustees should evaluate how the investment manager meets the purpose and objectives set forth in plan investment policy and guidelines (see page 56).

Trustees must also establish both the time horizon and benchmarks on which a manager bases reports to the trustees. Most trustees use a rolling three- to five-year time horizon to measure performance. Some of the more common benchmarks trustees use to monitor a manager's performance include:

- A broad-based stock market index, such as the Russell 3000 Index or the Wilshire

5000 Index. Large cap investments may be measured against large cap indices such as the S&P 500 or Russell 1000. Small cap investments may be measured against a small cap index such as the Russell 2000.

- International equity investments may be measured against a non-U.S. benchmark such as the MSCI EAFE (developed non-U.S. markets in Europe, Australasia and the Far East) or the MSCI All Country World ex-U.S. Index (developed and emerging non-U.S. markets). Global investment strategies (those that include both U.S. and non-U.S. investments) might be measured against a global index such the MSCI World Index.

- A bond market index that is comparable to the average portfolio maturity, sector composition and quality of the bonds in the trust portfolio. Examples are Barclays Capital U.S. Aggregate Bond Index, Barclays Capital U.S Treasury 1-3 Year Index, and Barclays Capital U.S. Long Government/Credit Index.

- A real estate index such as the NCREIF Property Index if the trust has private (not publicly traded) real estate investments. Publicly traded real estate investment trusts (REITs) might be measured against an index such as the Wilshire U.S. REIT Index.

- Barclays Capital U.S. Mortgage Backed Securities Index for mortgage investments

- Ryan Labs 3-Year GIC Index if the trust has guaranteed investment contracts

- A neutral or added-value benchmark such as a commercial paper index or the 91-day Treasury Bill Index to measure minimum performance levels. This benchmark measures how much additional value the investment manager provided over the simplest, lowest risk investments available. Consider developing an expected "premium" over a low-risk benchmark for a given investment strategy such as "91-day T-bills + 3%." Such benchmarks will likely be more useful for longer term comparisons.

- Another added-value index can be any index mutual fund from the financial page

✔ Meet with your plan's investment manager(s) and investment consultant to review the criteria used to monitor investment performance. Ask them to review the investment report for the last one-, three- and five-year periods, and compare the report to your plan's measurement criteria.

✔ Do not evaluate an investment manager on a short time horizon. Every investment has a cycle with positive, stable and negative returns. If an investment manager is following trustee investment guidelines and the discipline of his or her own investment style (e.g., value or growth), you should not be overly concerned with gains and losses for three or six months. Evaluate the manager's total performance over a three- to five-year time horizon.

✔ If your plan has two investment managers who utilize different investment styles, do not compare them as in a horse race (e.g., who comes in first). A contest against each other is both counterproductive and detrimental. The different investment styles should add to the total diversification and, over the long term, complement each other. When one investment style is in favor, the other style may not be. This adds balance to plan investment objectives.

✔ When selecting an investment manager, do not base the selection solely on who had the best past performance. The investment style that produced the best past performance may be out of favor during the next business cycle. Select an investment manager based on his or her ability to meet investment objectives and guidelines over a long-term time horizon.

✔ Don't be concerned with average performance on an annual basis. Look for long-term consistency and stability versus home runs.

of the newspaper. Anyone can invest money in a stock or bond index mutual fund. This benchmark will measure what additional value the plan's investment manager provided over a commercial index fund that an average person with no investment talent or experience could achieve.

- The Consumer Price Index or other price index to measure inflation. This helps determine what the *real rate of return* is—the return minus inflation. If the investment return is 8% and inflation is 3%, the real rate of return is 5%.

Evaluation of an investment manager's performance must take into consideration the economic circumstances of the marketplace. For example, if the S&P 500 Index is -10% and the investment manager's stock performance is -8%, the manager's performance is probably satisfactory. However, if the manager's stock performance is 1% when the S&P 500 Index is -10%, trustees should ask why. On the surface this appears to be good news, but the manager may be taking excessive risk or investing too much in one market sector or security to achieve spectacular investment performance.

When trustees evaluate an investment manager's performance, ideally, it should be *net of fees*. If the investment manager's return is 8%, and the management fee is 50 basis points, the return net of fees is 7.5% (8% − .5%).

Most multiemployer funds use the services of an investment consultant to monitor the performance of investment managers. The consultant provides advice on the best time horizons and benchmarks to use for monitoring performance. For example, trustees do not want to use a long-term bond index if a fund portfolio has short-term bonds. An investment consultant also has access to performance results for many investment managers across the United States and can compare the performance of your manager to other managers. A consultant can also provide invaluable help in assessing the appropriateness of the manager's fees.

Defined Benefit Pension Plans: Investment Assumptions

Actuaries make assumptions as to what investment earnings will be in the future. These assumptions are part of the annual actuarial report and are critical to properly funding a pension plan. If the investment assumptions (and all other assumptions) are met, a defined benefit pension plan will have sufficient assets to meet pension obligations. The investment assumption must be met over the long term. For example, if an actuarial investment assumption is a 7% return, actual investment return does not need to be exactly 7% each and every year. Investment earnings must average 7% over the period of time the actuary has selected.

Health and Welfare Plans: Investment and Reserve Policies

Health and welfare trustees should have a policy concerning plan reserves. The proper amount of reserves is a balance between meeting legal obligations, providing short-term benefits and maintaining long-term benefit stability. Chapter 2 offers further discussion on establishing health and welfare benefit plan reserves.

Once a reserve policy has been established, trustees should develop an investment policy as to how the reserves will be managed. The policy should seek to maximize return while protecting reserves from the risk of loss. Maintaining liquidity for the payment is also important. *Liquidity* is the ability to convert assets into cash quickly without a significant loss in value.

A health and welfare plan investment policy divides reserve assets into several categories. Each category has a different time horizon and may be invested differently.

- One-quarter to one-third of reserves are maintained indefinitely to meet legal obligations if the plan should terminate. If the plan is in a stable or growing industry, these assets may be invested over a longer time horizon such as five to ten years. There is less need for liquidity.
- One-quarter to one-half of reserves are kept available to stabilize benefits during a temporary industry downturn. Industry economics and historical patterns will dictate the time horizon and liquidity needs. These assets may be invested over a time horizon of two to five years.

✔ Ask your plan administrator to show you the most recent administrative financial report. Identify the amounts in the restricted and unrestricted reserves and ask why each amount is needed.

✔ Ask your plan administrator what your trust investment policy is and what the investment return has been.

✔ Evaluate how much income is produced from plan investments and what level of benefits this provides participants. If the reserves are invested as one pooled account, ask whether the reserves could be divided into several accounts based upon the liquidity needs of the plan.

✔ Meet with your plan administrator and actuary or health insurance consultant. Ask for an explanation of future benefit projections and administrative costs.

✔ Ask your plan actuary to review the interest assumptions and time horizons used. Discuss with the actuary what would happen if the trust averaged 1% less or 1% more than the assumed investment assumption for a ten-year period. For example, what would happen if the average return is 6% or 8% compared to the assumed 7%? Follow up by asking what contribution level would be necessary to make up a 1% shortfall, and what level of benefit increase could be made with a 1% gain?

✔ Meet with the investment advisor for your plan and ask how the investment return on reserves could be improved by 50 or 100 basis points (0.5% or 1%). Ask if increasing the yield would increase risk or cause problems with cash flow needs.

• One-quarter to one-third of reserves are used regularly to stabilize benefits during a normal seasonal cycle for the industry (e.g., high-summer and low-winter employment in the construction industry). Industry history will dictate the time horizon such as six months to one year, and liquidity needed.

Common Investment Mistakes Trustees Make

Mistake #1: Assuming the investment manager that performed the best this year will perform the best in the future. The following example illustrates how markets change and that different markets favor different investment styles and strategies. Assume large cap growth assets returned 12% last year.

Manager X reports that his firm's small cap stock portfolio returned 22%. He encourages transferring some plan assets from large cap growth stocks to small cap stocks.

Manager Y from another investment firm reports that her firm's return on value stocks was 6.5% last year. She suggests reducing the allocation in value stocks and increasing the allocation to large cap growth stocks.

While X recommends reducing investments in large cap growth stocks, Y recommends exactly the opposite. Keep in mind that markets change. A plan's investment policy and asset allocation is designed to maintain viability over the long term in different markets and business cycles. Follow the advice of your investment consultant.

Mistake #2: Not rebalancing the trust's portfolio. Assume that a trust allocation to large cap U.S. equities is $1 million and the return last year was 20%. Also, assume that the allocation to small cap equities is $1 million and last year's return was 2%. The large cap portfolio now has $1.2 million ($1 million × .20) and the small cap allocation has $1.02 million ($1 million × .02). The portfolio needs to be rebalanced so the large cap and the small cap portfolios both have $1.11 million ($1.2 million + 1.02 million ÷ 2).

Trustees must resist the temptation to not rebalance because it is taking dollars from the best performer and giving the dollars to the poor performer. The performance was last year. Your investment policy and asset allocation should emphasize maintaining viability over the long term in different economic situations.

Mistake #3: Basing an investment firm's capabilities on the personality of an individual. An investment management firm is made up of many individuals and departments. The most important aspect of the firm is the investment style that you hired the firm to perform. Listen to your investment consultant. If the consultant reports the firm has started to deviate from the style you hired it for, you need to take action.

The person from the investment firm who communicates with trustees is always going to paint the best picture on behalf of the firm. If a principal of a firm leaves, the firm is always going to say the firm has adequate backup. If the firm starts taking more risk, your manager will say it is designed to make you more money. As a trustee, it is your duty to ask questions that will reveal what is really happening.

Common Questions and Answers

1. **How many investment managers should we have for our multiemployer trust fund?**

   There is no established number or magic formula. The number depends on the objectives for and investment policy of your plan.

   Most multiemployer pension plans use more than one investment manager for expertise, diversification or both. Having two investment managers with different styles can help diversify your plan's total portfolio and risk. For example, hire a growth-style manager who invests in established companies with the potential for long-term capital appreciation, and a value manager who focuses on price/earnings ratios and book values of companies. If you want to allocate 10% of your trust portfolio to real estate investments, select an investment manager who specializes in real estate investments, has an excellent reputation and has demon-

strated above-average returns for this type of investment.

Health and welfare plans normally have one investment manager who has expertise in achieving good returns with stable, low-risk investment vehicles. A large health and welfare fund, however, may have two or more investment managers.

Trustees should periodically review plan investment objectives with the assistance of a neutral, independent investment consultant. Keep in mind that very few investment managers will suggest that you should retain the services of another investment manager. An independent investment consultant can assist you in determining whether another investment manager will enhance investment return, provide better diversification of risk, or both.

As a new trustee, you will receive numerous solicitations from investment managers (and other professionals) who want to do business with your trust. A trust normally has a policy on solicitations, such as referring the solicitor to the investment consultant or another consultant who assists trustees with investments. Find out what the policy on solicitation is for your plan and follow it.

2. **May a plan limit real estate investments to only union construction projects?**

   This is sometimes called *social investing* or *economically targeted investments (ETIs)*. The trustees' fiduciary responsibility is to invest trust assets to provide retirement income for participants and their beneficiaries.

   The U.S. Department of Labor (DOL) has maintained a consistent position regarding trustee fiduciary duty under ERISA (Sections 403(c) and 404(a)), and investing in ETIs. DOL's position (Interpretive Bulletin 94-1) provides that a fiduciary may not cause a plan to invest in an instrument with a lower rate of return or greater risk when there are similar investments with a greater rate of return that have equal or lower risk. Trustees may not substitute increased contributions to a plan or other collateral benefit to a plan to justify a lower rate of return or greater investment risk. This means trustees cannot use investing in companies that will provide jobs for union members to justify a lower rate of return or added risk when there are more favorable investment opportunities available. DOL's position states that if the return and risk requirements are met first, and there is also a social value, then trustees are allowed to make the investment.

If you consider an ETI, obtain the services of a competent advisor who has expertise in the type of investment (e.g., real estate, bank loans, municipal bonds) being considered. The advisor should be completely independent and have absolutely no political or financial stake in the outcome. The advisor can compare the return and risk relationship of the proposed investment to other investment opportunities. Ask the trust attorney for advice on ERISA fiduciary responsibility and the liability of trustees in relationship to the proposed investment and the independent advisor's report. Remember, trustees who violate the fiduciary standard for an ETI are personally liable for any loss.

3. **We have one investment manager who is performing well and one who is average. Should we replace the average manager?**

Don't make a horse race out of performance between your investment managers. The key is to determine if both managers are complying with your plan objectives, purpose and investment guidelines. If the answer is "yes," then both investment managers are performing satisfactorily. If the managers are performing in accordance with the investment guidelines and you do not like the outcome, you have to evaluate whether your plan's investment policy, asset allocation and diversification are accomplishing your investment objectives.

There may be several reasons for a difference between managers. First, the managers may have different investment styles. If one uses a growth style and the other a value style, the current market may favor one style over another. Have your plan investment consul-

✔ *Ask your plan administrator what your plan's policy is on solicitations from investment managers, and be sure you follow it.*

✔ *Understand each professional advisor's report concerning your plan and ask questions if there are any differences. The "whys" are very important in your duty to monitor the performance of professional advisors.*

✔ *Keep in mind that the period used to measure investments can dramatically affect a report on investment return.*

tant compare your investment manager to other managers who use the same style.

Having an investment manager who is the top performer in a given year may or may not be desirable for trustees. If an investment manager has outperformed the market and other managers in a style group, determine why. Is the performance due to the manager changing his or her style or exceeding the risk guidelines? Has the manager overweighted a sector of the economy (e.g., durable goods, energy, technology) beyond his or her normal style to produce the favorable result? If an investment manager overweights a sector, he or she has increased risk.

Remember that increases in risk can produce both favorable and unfavorable returns. Just because the manager's investment return is very favorable for the current reporting period does not mean you should not review the manager's overall performance and conformance with your trust investment policy and guidelines. An investment consultant is very helpful in evaluating performance, style and risk from a neutral perspective.

4. **The actuary, custodian bank, investment manager and investment consultant all report a different rate of investment return for last year. Why is this and who should we believe?**

Ask why the reports of these four professionals are different. If the explanation is logical and reasonable, you can rely on all of the reports. One reason the reports may be different is that each professional uses a different time frame, such as a "plan year" compared to a "calendar year," to measure investment results. Another reason is that the custodian bank, the investment manager and the investment consultant may use different methods to determine the market value of the assets. If June 1 is the measuring point, one professional advisor may have calculated the market value at the beginning of the day and the other may have used the market value at the end of the day. The market value of stocks and bonds can have a significant change in value during one day. In addition, some investments (e.g., real estate) do not have a determinable value on a day-to-day basis. Your professionals may be using a different valuation method or service to value or rate a real estate investment.

The investment manager, custodian bank and investment consultant normally use the actual market value of the asset on a particular date. In contrast, the actuary may use an averaging method to smooth investment gains and losses. The investment return reported by the actuary, therefore, may be an average of this year's investment return with those from the previous two years. An actuary who averages investment returns will always have a different investment return when compared to the other advisors.

Using the audited report of your plan is one way to obtain a reliable snapshot of annual investment return. This report is what your plan administrator must use when filing the annual Form 5500 with the federal government.

5. **Our pension trust had a 20% investment return last year, and the actuarial assumption is 7%. Can we spend the additional 13% on benefit improvements?**

Remember that investment returns should be viewed over the long term and not on a year-to-year basis. If the investment return last year was minus 10%, would you want to decrease benefits? Probably not.

Investment returns have ups and downs, peaks and valleys. Over a long-term period, investments should equal the actuary's investment assumption rate. If the investment return over a five- or ten-year period exceeds the actuarial assumption, the actuary will advise you on the feasibility of benefit increases.

6. **What is a trustee's responsibility for proxy voting?**

This is sometimes referred to as *corporate governance*. The U.S. Department of Labor (DOL) has issued an interpretive bulletin setting forth its opinion on how ERISA's fiduciary provisions apply to proxy voting. The responsibility of voting proxies is part of the fiduciary duty of managing plan assets.

Trustees normally delegate this responsibility to an investment manager. If you delegate this authority, you must still monitor performance of the duty. A provision in your plan investment guidelines should require that the investment manager keep a record of proxy voting and report votes to trustees on a periodic basis. Ask your plan attorney to assist you in developing procedures to comply with the DOL interpretive bulletin on proxy voting.

CHAPTER 5

Administration

You and your fellow trustees establish the administrative policies that achieve the purpose and objectives of a multiemployer plan. Most plans use the services of a professional administrator to implement these policies and to perform the day-to-day administrative functions required to provide benefits to participants and their dependents.

If you and your fellow trustees elect to increase the maximum annual dental benefit from $2,000 to $2,500 per year and you want to notify each participant by mail, you must rely on your plan administrator to have accurate enrollment records and current mailing addresses for all participants. The administrator, with the assistance of your plan's consultants and legal counsel, will draft the letter notifying participants of the benefit increase. The administrator is also responsible for finalizing, printing and mailing the letter. After receiving the letter, participants with questions about the change will contact the administrator for answers. In this example, the administrator is also responsible for amending the summary plan description (SPD) to incorporate the dental benefit increase.

A plan administrator may be a person directly employed by a trust fund (called a *salaried administrator*). Alternatively, trustees can contract with an independent or *third-party administrator (TPA)*.

Trustee Responsibility

ERISA places the fiduciary responsibility to administer a multiemployer plan upon trustees. The plan must be administered in accordance with plan documents as well as all relevant laws and regulations. Some of these administrative responsibilities are:

- Establish the content of plan documents, including updates and modifications to comply with legal changes and amendments made by trustees. The trust attorney and other professional advisors can assist in drafting and amending plan documents.
- Establish eligibility rules for participation in the plan.
- Establish benefit levels consistent with the financial resources of the plan.
- Communicate with plan participants and their dependents so they know who is eligible for plan benefits, what the benefits are and how the benefits are obtained.
- As appropriate, establish any reciprocity agreements with other trust funds that address eligibility, benefit credit and transfer of contributions. For example, some construction industry multiemployer funds have an agreement with other construction industry multiemployer funds to maintain a member's benefit coverage in the plan sponsored by the home local, even though the

person is temporarily employed in another multiemployer fund jurisdiction.

- Provide participants with all notices required by law in a timely manner. Such notices include COBRA notices in a health and welfare plan, and the annual funding notice for a multiemployer pension plan.
- Select the person(s) and organization(s) that will provide benefit services. In a health and welfare plan, service providers may include hospitals, physicians, insurance carriers, HMOs, PPOs, dental and vision providers, pharmacy benefit managers, etc.
- Select and monitor the performance of advisors and plan professionals (e.g., attorney, actuary, auditor, investment manager, insurance consultant and administrator).
- Select the depository for and custodian of trust assets—normally a custodian bank.
- Establish investment policy for trust assets.
- Monitor contributing employer compliance with the collective bargaining agreement(s) and participation agreement(s). Establish a delinquency procedure to enforce compliance.
- Establish a procedure for participants to appeal a denial of benefits. Trustees must review each appeal and make an appropriate decision based on the policy established in trust documents. See page 85 for more information concerning the claim appeals process.
- Assure each required government report (e.g., Form 5500) is properly completed and filed in a timely manner.
- Monitor all administrative activities to ensure they comply with the collective bargaining agreement, trust document, trustee policy, and applicable laws and regulations.
- Comply with all bonding and insurance obligations required by law and prudence.
- Maintain complete and accurate minutes of all trustee meetings and decisions.

Functions of the Administrator

Trustees delegate the day-to-day administrative functions of a plan. An administrator is usually asked to:

- Act as custodian of trust documents, records and property with proper security and control.
- Manage or employ a competent, well-trained staff that performs day-to-day administrative duties.
- Process the enrollment of plan participants and their dependents; act as custodian of participant data (e.g., dependent status, designated beneficiary, dates of birth, claims data) with proper security and control.
- Determine the current eligibility of enrolled participants and dependents by applying trust eligibility rules.
- Maintain an ongoing record of eligible participants and dependents, and report their eligibility to benefit providers and claims payers (e.g., medical insurance company, PPO or HMO).
- Ensure there is proper communication with participants regarding benefit eligibility, benefit levels and how to obtain benefits.
- Accept and process applications for benefits and make benefit payments as appropriate. In a pension plan, the administrator processes participant retirement applications and pays the monthly pension annuity checks to retirees. In a health and welfare plan, the administrator receives a claim from the participant or health care service provider and pays the appropriate amount.
- Process any benefit claim appeals according to the plan's written claims appeal procedure.
- Collect contribution payments from employers and self-payments from participants (e.g., COBRA premiums), then make sure the money collected is properly deposited and used to pay the normal and reasonable expenses of the plan.
- Process and account for contributions as required by the trust documents, collective bargaining agreement(s) and participation agreement(s).
- Report to trustees on the status of plan assets, income and expenses. This is typically a monthly or quarterly financial statement.

- Implement the trust delinquency procedure to enforce collection of employer contributions.
- Arrange trustee meetings (e.g., meeting facilities, notices) and perform the administrative functions at the meeting (e.g., take minutes) as directed by the trustees.
- Make sure the plan fulfills all meeting requirements contained in the trust documents (e.g., quorum).
- Make sure all required government reports are complete and filed in a timely manner.
- Make sure all notices required by law are properly sent to participants.
- Administer the HIPAA privacy policy and rules.
- Perform other duties as delegated by the trustees.

Key Documents for Plan Administration

As explained in Chapter 1, trustees have a fiduciary duty to administer the plan in conformance with plan documents, and to comply with all laws and regulations. The following documents are essential to administration of a multiemployer trust.
- Trust document(s). See page 7.
- Plan document or SPD. See page 8.
- Collective bargaining agreement. See page 8.
- Minutes of trust meetings. See page 8.
- IRS determination letter. See page 9.
- Investment policy. See page 56.
- Custodian report. See page 68.
- Administrator's report. See the next section on this page.
- Audited financial statements. See Chapter 6, which begins on page 93.
- Form 5500. Submitted to the federal government annually, the Form 5500 reports the number of plan participants, plan amendments (if any were made), trust funding, types of plan benefits, the plan's professional advisor(s) and service providers along with any payments made to them, and the opinions of the actuary and auditor. Fines and penalties can result if Form 5500 is filed late or is incomplete.

The Administrator's Report

The administrator processes the monthly contribution and work units reports submitted by employers to determine participant eligibility. While it is becoming increasingly rare among multiemployer plans, some administrators deposit employer contributions into the trust account at the custodian bank. Today, employer contributions for most plans are sent directly to the custodian bank. The administrator may also receive and deposit self-payments made by plan participants.

Employer contribution reports contain important information trustees need to manage a plan. The administrator should summarize the information in these reports and make it available to trustees on a monthly or quarterly basis. Items that may be included in the administrator's report are:
- The number of participants in the plan. This can be further broken down into actives, dependents, nonworking participants who retain coverage, retirees, surviving spouses, etc.
- The average number of hours worked and/or amount of contribution received per eligible participant and reported participant. An *eligible participant* works sufficient hours to obtain coverage under the plan's eligibility rules. A *reported participant* is anyone who worked one or more hours during the reporting period, including persons who have not worked sufficient hours to be eligible under plan rules. If the plan has more reported participants than eligible participants, the contributions made on behalf of the noneligible participants are called *breakage*. The amount of breakage is very important in funding benefits given to eligible participants, because the contributions for reported ineligible participants help fund benefits for eligible participants.
- The number of hours being credited to an hours bank, if an hours bank is used. Also, the amount of reserve necessary to meet the hours bank liability.
- Administrative costs, which may include administrative fees and the cost of pro-

fessional advisors (e.g., attorney(s), accountant(s), custodian bank, investment manager(s)).

- A financial statement that shows all income and expenses for the plan for the past month and quarter. This statement also shows all plan assets held by a custodian bank. See question 1 on page 89 for additional discussion on the administrator's report.

Eligibility Rules for Health and Welfare Plans

Every multiemployer health and welfare plan must have written rules that determine who is eligible to participate in the plan. Every plan must also have rules that determine when coverage terminates. Trustees establish these rules, which must be communicated to plan participants in the summary plan description (SPD) and SBC (summary of benefit coverage). The plan administrator administers the rules. Common eligibility rules include:

- **Waiting period for new participants.** The waiting period occurs between the date of hire with a participating employer and the date the participant and dependents are first eligible for benefits under a plan. If Mary is hired on March 1 and is eligible for plan benefits on May 1, the plan has a two-month waiting period. The purpose of a waiting period is normally to prevent selectivity against the plan. Trustees do not want an employer hiring her brother-in-law on Monday so he is eligible for expensive elective surgery on Tuesday. Although not common, the length of a waiting period can be different for participants and dependents.
- **Hours-based eligibility.** Eligibility is based on the number of hours a participant must work in a month (or the hours for which the employer contributes) to maintain trust-paid coverage. If a multiemployer plan has an 80-hour-per-month eligibility rule, Jack is eligible if he works 80 or more hours in May, but he is not eligible if he works less than 80 hours. Some plans use a month or other period of time rather than hours to

determine eligibility. A participant may be eligible if he or she works any time during the month. Or, a participant may be eligible for coverage in the next calendar quarter if he or she works during the previous calendar quarter.

- **Continued trust eligibility for a non-working participant.** Some multiemployer plans have special eligibility rules that continue plan-paid coverage for participants who are on layoff, are affected by seasonal employment patterns, or have an industrial injury or other disability. Many plans provide for this continued coverage through an hours bank. Other plans have an eligibility rule that a participant is covered for the entire year once he or she has worked at least six months during the year. Some plans have rules that a participant who is not working due to a disability or layoff has up to three months per year of continued plan-paid coverage. All group medical plans with 20 or more participants must permit continued coverage through COBRA (see question 3 on page 32).

Hours Bank

Many multiemployer health and welfare plans in seasonal or cyclical industries use an hours bank to provide eligibility when a participant is not working. An hours bank works in this way:

- Trustees establish the minimum hours an employee must work (or minimum contributions received) in a month (or other period) to receive trust-paid coverage. For example, an employee must work 120 hours per month.
- When an employee works in excess of the minimum hours requirement, the surplus hours are credited to the employee's individual hours bank. If Sally works 160 hours in June and 120 hours are required for eligibility, 40 hours will be credited to Sally's hours bank account.
- When an employee does not work the minimum number of hours in a month for eligibility, the employee can draw upon his or her hours bank to meet the minimum

Table 5-I

Example of Hours Bank

Month	Hours Worked	Minimum Eligibility	Hours Bank Account
June	160	120	40
July	170	120	90
August	150	120	120
September	140	120	140
October	100	120	120
November	0	120	0

requirements. If Sally works 80 hours in November, she can draw 40 hours from her hours bank to meet the 120-hour eligibility requirement.

In the example shown in Table 5-I, Sally builds up her hours bank in June through September and draws from the bank for eligibility in October and November. Be aware that if the plan has a one lag month system, the October and November eligibility from the hours bank provides actual coverage in December and January.

Lag Months

Most multiemployer health and welfare plans operate on a one or two *lag month* system. In a one lag month system, employer contributions made for hours worked during the month of January might determine eligibility for the month of March. January hours and contributions are reported by employers to the plan administrator in February (e.g., by the tenth or 15th day of the month). The plan administrator uses the remainder of February to process the employer reports, determine participant eligibility and notify the claims payer which participants are eligible for benefits in March.

Determining Eligibility for Health and Welfare Plans

The administrator's function is to ensure that benefits are properly delivered to eligible participants and their dependents. The following is a walk-through of a typical administrative process to determine eligibility in a multiemployer health and welfare plan.

- Individuals must be given a copy of the SBC when they are first eligible to enroll in a health plan, during open enrollment and upon request.
- Employees complete a plan enrollment card to enroll themselves and their dependents in the plan. Important enrollment data for each participant and dependent are name, age, address, employer and Social Security number. In the enrollment process for a health plan, the participant may also be asked to identify any other group insurance plan his or her dependents participate in that is needed for the coordination of benefits. For life insurance and other death

Tips for New Trustees

✔ *Make sure you clearly understand the lag month system, especially if you are in a cyclical industry. A person who does not work sufficient hours in January will not be affected for two or three months.*

✔ *Meet with your plan administrator and review how lag months coordinate with COBRA, an hours bank or other continued eligibility systems.*

benefits the participant is asked to designate his or her beneficiary.

- Participants must be given a copy of a plan's latest SPD when they first become covered by a plan and at regular intervals thereafter.
- New health plan participants must also be given a copy of the initial COBRA notice.
- Employers submit monthly contribution reports to the administrator for processing.
  - These reports list each employee who works under the labor agreement and the number of hours each employee worked during the month reported.
  - Based upon hours worked, the administrator determines whether each participant has met eligibility requirements for plan-paid coverage.
  - An employee who has not worked sufficient hours to meet plan eligibility requirements is afforded the opportunity to maintain eligibility through an hours bank (if the trust uses such a procedure). When there is no hours bank, an ineligible participant and dependents are notified of their right to continue medical coverage through COBRA. A participant whose eligibility is interrupted by military service is eligible for extended coverage under USERRA. Participants may also continue coverage during FMLA leave.
  - A list of all eligible employees is provided to the organization that pays claims (e.g., the insurance carrier, HMO, PPO).
- The administrator audits employer contribution reports to ensure the monetary payment is correct relative to the hours reported and contribution rate required by the collective bargaining agreement. Contributions are deposited in the custodian bank.
- The administrator responds to questions from participants regarding benefits and eligibility.
- The administrator processes any dependent eligibility under court orders or a state law. For example, a qualified medical child support order (QMCSO) mandates that a plan provide coverage for a child of a noncustodial parent who is a plan participant.

- If the administrator also pays claims, the administrator reports eligibility to service providers (e.g., doctors, hospitals) and processes claims submitted by these providers.

Determining Eligibility for Pension Plans

The following is the typical administrative process used by a multiemployer pension plan to determine eligibility.

- Participants enroll in the pension plan by completing a plan enrollment card. Important data provided includes the participant's name, date of birth, Social Security number and current address. If the participant is married, the spouse's name, age and Social Security number are requested. If the plan has a death benefit, an unmarried participant may name a beneficiary. If the plan has a reciprocity agreement with other pension plans or gives credit for industry service, the participant is asked to provide a work history.
- Each participant is given a copy of the plan SPD upon enrollment.
- The employer's monthly contribution report is processed. The hours each participant worked during the reporting period are credited to the employee's personal account to determine vesting and benefit credits.
- The administrator audits contribution reports to ensure monetary payments are consistent with the hours the employer reported and the contribution rate in the collective bargaining agreement. Contributions are deposited in the custodian bank.
- The plan administrator sends each participant a summary annual report that informs

the participant of the plan's financial status. Each participant also receives an annual benefit statement that states the participant's status and benefit rights. When amendments to a pension plan are made by trustees, participants are provided a written notice of the changes. Participants also receive an annual funding notice required by the Pension Protection Act (PPA).

- For a defined contribution (DC) pension plan where a participant can manage his or her own account, a fee disclosure is sent to the participant.
- The administrator responds to benefit and eligibility questions from participants and dependents.
- The administrator processes eligibility for benefits granted via a divorce or separation proceeding when the court issues a qualified domestic relations order (QDRO).

Reciprocity

Some multiemployer funds enter into reciprocity agreements with other trust funds in the same or similar industries—especially when the workforce is very mobile and participants often work for several different employers. Reciprocity is accomplished in one of several ways. Pension Fund A and Pension Fund B might agree to give reciprocity for vesting credits. Let's say that Mary works three years in Fund A and two years in Fund B. Under reciprocity, both Fund A and Fund B give Mary the full five years of pension vesting credit. However, Fund A gives Mary only three years of pension benefit credit, and Fund B gives Mary only two years of pension benefit credit.

A common health and welfare plan reciprocity arrangement is for Fund B to permit a participant to maintain health and welfare benefit eligibility under Fund A even though the person is working in Fund B's jurisdiction. Consider Bill who is a resident of Seattle, Washington and a participant in the Washington State Construction Workers' Plan. Bill travels with his employer, Heavy-Duty Construction Company, to work on a bridge construction project in Portland, Oregon. Even though Bill is working in the jurisdiction of the

Oregon Construction Workers' Plan, the Oregon plan permits Heavy-Duty Construction to submit contributions on behalf of Bill to the Washington State plan. The Washington plan pays all benefit claims submitted by Bill and his dependents.

For Oregon union members hired by Heavy-Duty Construction to work on the Portland construction project, the contractor submits contributions to the Oregon plan. For some reciprocity agreements, the contractor submits all contributions to the local plan, and the local plan administrator sends the contributions to the employee's home plan.

If an Oregon plan participant travels to Washington for a construction job, the Washington plan permits the Oregon participant to continue coverage under the Oregon plan through the same reciprocal agreement.

Benefit Payments for Health and Welfare Plans

Health and welfare trustees determine the level of benefits a plan will provide to eligible participants and their dependents. Trustees delegate the administration of these benefit payments to a *claims payer,* which may be the plan administrator, an insurance carrier or a service provider (e.g., an HMO or PPO). The procedure on how to file a claim is communicated to the participants and their dependents in the SPD.

The procedure for paying claims is relatively simple. The plan issues every participant and dependent an identification card and number. The participant gives his or her plan identification number to the doctor, pharmacist, hospital or other health care provider. The provider often will contact the plan administrator or claims payer to determine whether the participant is eligible for benefits. If eligible, the provider renders the good or service to the participant (e.g., the pharmacy provides prescription drugs) and submits the bill to the claims payer. The claims payer reviews the billing, remits the appropriate payment to the provider and sends a statement to the participant. The statement explains what services were covered, amounts paid, amounts not paid and why. The statement also informs the participant to whom he or she may direct questions, and how to submit an appeal if the participant believes there were errors or the claim was not properly paid.

In most multiemployer plans, the claims payer has a procedure for *coordination of benefits (COB)* with other group medical plans. The COB procedure must be described in the SPD. The following example illustrates a COB procedure. Assume Mary, who is a participant in Plan A, is married to Jack and has a son, Eddie. Jack and Eddie are enrolled as Mary's dependents in Plan A. Further, assume Jack is employed and is a participant of Plan B. Jack lists Mary and Eddie as his dependents in Plan B. Eddie, a junior in high school, has limited medical coverage provided by the high school's athletic insurance policy for injuries incurred playing high-school football. Assume Eddie breaks his leg catching the winning touchdown pass in the state high-school championship game. Who pays the medical claims for Eddie's broken leg—Plan A, Plan B or the high-school insurance policy?

The rules determining which medical insurance plan pays Eddie's claim are normally controlled by state insurance laws. The claims payer is responsible for identifying all of the group insurance coverages that Eddie is eligible to receive and to coordinate the payment of Eddie's

claim according to the state rules. Let's say that state law establishes Plan A as the *primary carrier,* which means Plan A pays Eddie's claim up to Plan A benefit limits. Plan B and the high-school insurance are considered *secondary payers* and split the remainder of Eddie's claim up to but not exceeding 100% of the total claim cost. If Eddie's claim is $2,000 and Plan A is an 80%/20% benefit policy, Plan A would pay $1,600 (.80 × $2,000). Plan B and the high-school football insurance would coordinate and pay the remaining $400 (.20 × $2,000). The claims payer for Plan A has the duty to coordinate benefits.

Benefit Payments for Pension Plans

Pension trustees establish the type and level of benefits a plan provides if it is not already dictated by a collective bargaining agreement or the law. A retirement benefit may be a fixed annuity, a lump-sum cash payment or a combination of the two. The SPD provides the details of what the plan's benefits are and what eligibility requirements (e.g., age, number of credits) a participant must meet to obtain benefits. The administrative duties that trustees of multiemployer pension plans typically delegate to an administrator include:

- If a DC plan allows a participant to borrow from his or her account before retirement age, the administrator processes the application, makes the payment and performs the recordkeeping. Be aware that the option to borrow from a plan is strictly controlled by IRS rules.
- When a participant applies for retirement, the administrator determines the person's eligibility and calculates the benefits. The application process normally involves the

---

Tips for New Trustees

✔ *Meet with your plan administrator and review how health and welfare claims are filed, processed and paid. Ask how COB is administered and the amount your plan saves by using a COB procedure.*

---

participant submitting documents proving age and marital status. If the participant applies for a disability pension, a medical certification of the disability must be provided. If a spouse or beneficiary applies for a death benefit, a death certificate is necessary.

- A defined benefit (DB) plan may have a number of benefit alternatives that a participant and spouse may select. As discussed in Chapter 3, options for a DB plan may include a normal life annuity based upon the life of the participant, a joint and survivor (J&S) annuity based on the life spans of both the participant and spouse, as well as other options. In a DC plan, the participant may be able to elect a lump-sum payment or combine a lump-sum payment with an annuity. The administrator is responsible for communicating all of the options available to the participant.

- After the participant submits all the necessary documents and selects the retirement option(s) he or she desires, the administrator makes the payments. If the pension is an annuity, the payments are sent monthly to the retiree. In a DC plan, the lump sum is paid to the retiree. Some multiemployer plans send pension payment(s) directly to the participant's bank account if the participant selects this service.

- Some participants may be subject to a QDRO that divides the participant's retirement benefits as part of a divorce or separation proceeding. If the participant is subject to a QDRO, the administrator disburses the pension payments to both the retiree and the former spouse.

- The administrator withholds income tax from the retirement payment(s) as directed by the retiree and submits withheld taxes to the appropriate federal and state tax collector. A pension trust may also permit retirees to elect other deductions from a pension check. For example, the retiree may elect to have his or her monthly payments for retiree medical coverage deducted from the pension annuity and sent directly to the health and welfare fund. The plan administrator

also handles these transactions.

- The administrator is responsible for monitoring retiree eligibility and terminating benefits according to plan rules. Reasons benefits may end include a retiree dies, a retiree returns to work at a participating employer or a disabled retiree recovers.

Tips for New Trustees

✔ *Review the pension application form(s) and put it in your trustee notebook.*

✔ *Meet with your plan administrator and review the retirement application process, what retirement options are available to participants and how the administrator communicates these options to participants. Also, examine how the administrator monitors retiree eligibility to ensure payments are not made after eligibility ends.*

Claim Appeals

Participants' Rights

The SPD must tell participants how to file an appeal if a benefit claim is denied. When there is a denial, the claims payer or administrator must provide the participant with the following in writing:

- The specific reason for the claim denial
- The section and page in the SPD providing the information upon which the denial is based
- Any information or material necessary for the participant to be eligible for payment or to complete the claim, and why this material is necessary
- An explanation of the plan appeal procedures.

Appealing a claim has several steps that must occur within specific time limits established by federal regulation. There are two sets of time limits for the appeal process. The first set has very short time limits for life-threatening procedures where the denial may prevent the person from obtaining medical care or treatment. Perhaps a plan excludes payment for nonnetwork hospitals except in an emergency and a plan participant needs an immediate heart operation—The physician says the participant cannot be moved from the nonnetwork to the closest network hospital, which is 100 miles away. In this example, the life-threatening appeal procedure and time limits apply.

The second set of time limits is for a non-life-threatening procedure or claim. A plan covers 50 miles of ambulance service and the participant used ambulance service for a 100-mile trip. The participant is now appealing the nonpayment of the additional 50 miles. In this case, the non-life-threatening appeal procedure and time limits apply. The plan attorney will advise trustees on the procedure and time limits established by law. Be aware that multiemployer plans can use a special appeals procedure that matches the timing of appeals with quarterly trustee meetings.

Under ERISA, a participant has the right to request and review (or receive) copies of plan documents, insurance contracts, the collective bargaining agreement and government filings (e.g., Form 5500) at no charge. If the participant does not receive the requested materials within 30 days, the participant may be awarded $110 a day by the court. The participant may file a lawsuit or seek assistance from the U.S. Department of Labor in any claim appeal. The SPD must also inform participants of these ERISA rights.

Processing Appeals

Trustees of many multiemployer plans appoint a claims appeal committee to review appeals at the first step of the claims procedure. This committee is normally made up of a management and union trustee, the plan administrator, a health care consultant, a representative of the claims payer and the plan attorney.

Most health and welfare claim appeals are processed very quickly because the participant or dependent is clearly not eligible, the medical procedure is not covered, there is a benefit cap permitted by the Patient Protection and Affordable Care Act of 2010 (ACA) or the proper documentation was not submitted. Perhaps the plan

covers dependent children until age 26, and the parent files a claim on a child after the child's 26th birthday. Alternatively, there might be a $2,000 annual cap on dental benefits and the participant appeals the nonpayment of $500 on a $2,500 dental claim. In another scenario, the participant's physician didn't submit documentation to verify the medical treatment was provided.

Most pension claim appeals are also processed very quickly because the participant is clearly not eligible or the proper documentation was not submitted. For example, retirement age for a plan is 65 and the participant applies at the age of 60. Or, the participant does not submit a birth certificate or other documents to verify age.

Occasionally, claim appeals become very technical. Assume a dental plan has a $2,000 annual cap. The participant (and physician) appeals that the $10,000 procedure (e.g., reconstructive surgery of the lower jaw) was medical rather than dental. Trustees must review the benefit terminology, limitations and other relevant provisions in the SPD. Trustees must rely upon the plan attorney and other professionals when making the decision.

In some cases, not following plan procedures set forth in the SPD creates financial hardship for a participant. Consider a participant who obtains preauthorization for three days in the hospital but stays a total of five days for nonmedical reasons. The plan pays for three days, and the hospital bills the participant for two days. The participant appeals the nonpayment for two hospital days. Trustees cannot make an "exception" for one participant and pay for two additional days contrary to the benefit schedule unless they are willing to make exceptions for *all* participants. Finally, ACA requires nongrandfathered plans to use enhanced appeal procedures and offer a participant external review rights for appeals involving medical necessity. An independent review organization will conduct the external review and render a decision that is binding on the plan.

Delinquency and Collection

Trustees have a fiduciary duty to collect contributions from employers participating in a plan. The plan administrator normally receives the contribution reports from the employer and is, therefore, the first to know whether the employer is making timely payments.

Trustees must establish a written collection procedure. The administrator, in coordination with the trust attorney, implements the collection process when necessary. The administrator keeps trustees informed of who is delinquent and the status of the collection.

The Trustee's Duty to Monitor the Administrator

Trustees have a fiduciary duty to monitor the performance of any individual or firm to whom they delegate responsibility. This duty includes monitoring the administrator. Trustees should clearly communicate directions and expectations to the administrator. If trustees delegate the preparation of a notice to participants, the trustees should be precise on the schedule for completing and sending the notice, including who will review the notice, who has authority to make changes and the deadlines for completion. Unless clear instructions and expectations are given, trustees cannot monitor performance.

Trustees should have a formal written agreement with the plan administrator setting forth the duties the trustees are delegating, the services desired and expectations. One provision in an administrative contract might state the administrator is responsible for properly submitting all government filings within the filing deadlines. Under this provision, the administrator holds the trustees harmless for any and all fines and penalties because of nonfilings and any incomplete,

improper or late filings. The plan attorney can assist trustees on the advisability of having an administrative contract and its content.

Trustees should periodically audit the performance of the administrator—a process sometimes referred to as an *operational audit*. The following is a list of items that trustees may want to include in an administrative audit.

Forms and Procedures
- ☐ A review of all enrollment forms and procedures. Is the enrollment procedure working? Are new participants being properly enrolled? Do participants enroll new dependents (e.g., through birth or marriage) in a timely manner?
- ☐ A review of employer reporting forms and procedures. Are employers complying?
- ☐ A review of health and welfare claims forms and pension application procedures. Are the procedures working? Are benefits accessible to participants and their dependents?
- ☐ Are all forms and procedures updated periodically to comply with changes in trustee policy and the law?
- ☐ Do local unions, company personnel managers or service providers report any concerns regarding the enrollment or claims procedures?

Employer Contributions and Reports
- ☐ Are contributions and reports complete, timely and accurate?
- ☐ Are contributions deposited properly?
- ☐ Are delinquency and collection procedures followed?
- ☐ What are the administrator's internal audit and control procedures?
- ☐ Does the plan auditor have any concerns?

Communication With Participants and Service Providers
- ☐ Are all ERISA communication mandates being complied with (e.g., SPD, SBC, summary annual report, benefit statements, claims denials, COBRA notices)?
- ☐ Does the administrative staff respond to written and verbal inquiries in a prompt,

professional manner? Have participants, union locals, company personnel managers or providers expressed any discontent?

Participant Data
- [ ] How does the administrator maintain records? Are they stored on paper or electronically? Are they in-house or contracted out?
- [ ] Does the administrator have and use up-to-date technology?
- [ ] Is participant data complete and accurate? Is it made available to other plan advisors in a timely and professional manner?
- [ ] Is there a complete and up-do-date name and address file for sending legal notices to participants?

Eligibility and Benefit Determinations
- [ ] Are eligibility and benefit determinations accurate? Is the administrator consistently and accurately applying plan standards and rules?
- [ ] What checks and balances does the administrator use to ensure benefits are properly calculated and paid? Is there an internal audit control system?
- [ ] Is the written claims appeal procedure being followed and are participants properly informed of their appeal rights? Are all appeals handled properly?
- [ ] Do the plan auditor, insurance consultant or actuary have any concerns?

Legal Compliance
- [ ] Is the administrator complying with all ERISA rules and regulations?
- [ ] Are all particpant disclosure requirements under COBRA, ACA, etc. being met?
- [ ] What procedures does the administrator use to ensure security and confidentiality to comply with HIPAA and other laws?
- [ ] Are all required government reporting forms being filed in a complete, accurate and timely manner?
- [ ] Does the plan legal counsel have any concerns?

Communication With Trustees
- [ ] Is the administrator accessible to trustees to resolve administrative issues and answer questions?
- [ ] Are trustees informed of claims appeals?
- [ ] Are trustees kept up-to-date on employer contributions, delinquencies and collections?
- [ ] Does the administrator keep trustees advised of how new federal and state laws will affect administration, and what it will cost to comply with these laws?
- [ ] Are administrative reports to trustees timely and accurate? Do they contain the necessary information for trustees to understand plan administration?
- [ ] Are meeting administrative duties performed satisfactorily (e.g., notice, meeting place)?
- [ ] Are the minutes of meetings complete, accurate and submitted in a timely manner?
- [ ] Does the plan attorney have any concerns?

Payment of Trust Expenses
- [ ] Are all trust expenses paid according to trust procedures? For example, are two signatures used as required by the trust agreement?
- [ ] Is there an internal audit and control procedure, and is it being followed?
- [ ] Does the administrative report advise trustees of each expense?
- [ ] Does the plan auditor or attorney have any concerns?

Trustee Protection
- [ ] Are all fidelity bonds in place with premiums paid?
- [ ] Is the fiduciary liability insurance policy adequate, and are all premiums paid?
- [ ] Does the plan attorney or insurance consultant have any concerns?

Administrative Service Costs

There is no such thing as a typical multiemployer plan administrator. It is difficult, therefore, for trustees to compare the cost of administrative services. What an administrator does for Plan A may be completely different from what an administrator does for Plan B. A plan administrator carries out the directions of the trustees and conforms his or her services to those directions. Multiemployer health and welfare Plan A might use an hours bank system while Plan B does not. The administrator for Plan A must maintain the recordkeeping system and employ staff to administer the hours bank. Plan B's administrator does not have this responsibility and staff cost. Administrative costs for the two plans, therefore, are completely different. Trustees must be sure that when they evaluate administrative costs, they are comparing apples to apples.

Trustees may want to consider periodically submitting administrative work for bid as a test of cost competitiveness and service adequacy. If an administrative agreement or contract is used, all the bidders submit bids on the requirements, duties and expectations contained in the contract.

ERISA-Prohibited Transactions for Unions and Associations Performing Administrative Services

ERISA prohibits both union and management entities that sponsor a plan from directly benefiting from trust assets. These entities can run afoul of the ERISA-prohibited transaction rules if they (1) perform administrative services for a multiemployer plan that are unnecessary to the purpose of the trust or (2) receive an unreasonable fee for performing a necessary service. Examples of prohibited transactions where the courts found trustees liable for improper use of trust assets for administrative services are:

- A union business representative who was also a plan trustee designed a one-sided contract—that only he could terminate—to make himself the plan administrator (*Gilliam v. Edwards* 1980).
- Trust assets were used to redecorate the common offices of the plan administrator and the union (*Marshal v. Snyder* 1978).

- A union trustee received compensation from a fund for encouraging employers to join or remain in the plan—This was not necessary to the plan (*McLaughlin v. Tomasso* 1988).
- Payments to union representatives for administrative services were made by the plan—No records were kept of time and duties (*Kim v. Fujikawa* 1989 and *Dole v. Formica* 1991).
- Trustees did not charge the sponsoring union reasonable rent in a trust-owned building (*Dole v. Formica* 1991).

Trustees should be very cautious and seek advice from legal counsel before entering into any administrative fee, service or rental agreement between a trust and either a management or union organization. If a service arrangement is appropriate, detailed and accurate records of time spent and services performed must be maintained. In office-sharing arrangements, an independent party should periodically advise trustees on the market rates for rent and clerical services, and trustees should get confirmation that the rates are properly charged. Before any administrative service agreement is made, the plan attorney should review the arrangement and advise trustees. Additional discussion of prohibited transactions is on page 5.

Common Questions and Answers

1. **Our administrator does not give us administrative reports. Should we get them?**
   Yes. Trustees have the ultimate fiduciary responsibility for proper administration. Administrative reports provide you with information on the financial status of your plan and other important administrative data. The basic information that trustees need includes:
   - [ ] Financial statement of income and expenses
     - Employer contributions
     - Contributions from other sources (e.g., self-payments)
     - Investment income
     - Realized investment gains and losses
     - Unrealized investment gains and losses

- Expenses
  - Administrative costs (e.g., fees, postage, phone)
  - Professional consultant fees for service (e.g., attorney, auditor, actuary)
  - Bank fees
  - Investment fees
  - Trustee meeting expenses
  - Insurance premiums, claims, etc.
  - Benefit payments
  - Other
- ☐ Financial statement of assets and liabilities
- ☐ Basic participant data
  - Number of participants
    - Actives
    - Retirees
    - Disabled
    - Laid off
    - COBRA
    - Dependents
  - Hours or units of contributions reported/made
  - Status of delinquent employers.

2. **Can our plan's administrative office be part of the union or trade association office?**

It is a prohibited transaction for trustees to cause plan assets to be paid to a "party in interest." Both the union and trade association are parties in interest. ERISA does provide an exemption for providing services to a trust if the services are necessary to carry out the purpose of the plan and the fees to provide the service are reasonable.

To properly assess this question, ask why it is necessary for the administrative office to be located in either the sponsoring union or trade association office complex.

- ☐ Is there a value or purpose that will actually benefit the participants (other than the benefit to the union or association)?
- ☐ If there is a true value to benefits participants, what is a reasonable rental fee?
- ☐ Is this rental fee in line with the market value of comparable rental property?
- ☐ Are there any residual questions? For example, will there be any other cost

sharing between the trust and the union or association (e.g., the sharing of a salary for a receptionist or sharing the costs of telephones, utilities, office equipment)?

Another ERISA-prohibited transaction section provides that trustees may not cause a trust to enter into a transaction with a party in interest. The U.S. Department of Labor position is that this provision prohibits trustees who have a direct interest in sharing office space to participate in the decision, even if the exemption criteria are met. For example, participants frequently visit a union office, hiring hall, etc. Assume participants will receive substantial advantage by having the administrative center located in the union office. In addition, the rental fee the union will charge the trust is 50% below market value. Even if all the exemption criteria are met, the DOL position is that union trustees cannot participate in making the decision.

Seek legal counsel before making any decision that involves a union or management organization directly related to administrative services. You may also want to seek a DOL exemption for the proposed service arrangement, to ensure full compliance with ERISA.

3. **How soon after a trustee meeting should trustees receive copies of minutes?**

Minutes are a very important record for trustees. Trustees should have the administrator prepare them as soon as possible after the meeting. This gives you and other trustees the opportunity to review the record of your actions and fiduciary considerations while memories are still fresh.

4. **Our administrator says that our health and welfare fund can save money by having him or her pay medical claims instead of the insurance carrier. Should we switch to the administrator?**

The payment of medical claims is a service that is necessary to carry out the purpose of a health and welfare plan. In this case, the insurance carrier and the administrator have competitive services. You have a fiduciary duty to delegate the claims payment service in the best interest of participants. The least expensive service, however, may not necessarily be the best. You have to look at all aspects of the service, including costs.

☐ What is the procedure participants have to follow to file a claim?

☐ Does the claims payer issue each participant an ID card that is accepted by medical providers, or does the participant have to complete a claim form?

☐ What are the claim procedures for an emergency when a participant is out of the area on vacation? What is the turnaround time on claims payments?

☐ How does each claims payer monitor coordination of benefits, and what is their experience on recovery?

☐ How does each claims payer handle denial of claims?

☐ What audit procedures does each claims payer have to assure there are no billing errors or fraud from medical providers?

These and many more questions have to be asked, answered and evaluated before making a decision. It is always helpful and prudent for trustees to obtain the assistance of a consultant or other advisor who has experience in asking the right questions and gathering the data to evaluate.

5. Can a plan administrator also be an investment advisor?

Assume a person associated with a plan, such as the plan administrator, a trustee, or participating employer, proposes plan assets be invested in a mall complex in which that person or organization is a partner. The investment opportunity is pitched as finding gold at the end of a rainbow.

In the majority of cases, when a person associated with a plan in one capacity wants to perform in another capacity, there is a legal issue or a prohibited transaction problem. ERISA has very stringent rules on whom trustees can use as professional advisors and with whom trustees can deal. You must be extremely careful when having a person or organization perform more than one service for a trust.

Keep in mind that a prohibited transaction imposes personal liability upon trustees. Ask your trust attorney to advise you on the ERISA-prohibited transaction and party-in-interest rules before you take any action.

6. Can pension benefits be stopped if a retiree returns to work for a nonunion contractor?

Trustees may adopt a plan provision that stops payment of pension benefits when a retiree returns to work. The provision must be in the SPD so participants and retirees have proper notice of the penalty for returning to work. Trustees, however, must balance the political and administrative issues of stopping a pension benefit.

As a trustee, you may not want to pay pension benefits to a participant who is working. But what is the definition of "return to work," and how does your plan enforce the provision? Is "work" defined as work within the same industry, or is it any gainful employment? The more rigid the definition, the more problems there will be with enforcement. If a plan uses "work within the same industry," can a carpenter who retires from a carpenter's pension fund in New York work as a carpenter in California? How will trustees in New York obtain sufficient information to enforce the rule on a retiree working in California?

Some industries traditionally call upon retirees to work temporarily for vacation or emergency relief. In these industries, a rule might be adopted that retirees can work within the industry for a minimum period such as 400 hours per year without loss of pension benefits.

There are a number of federal laws that affect the trustees' option to stop pension benefits if a retiree returns to work. For example, the National Labor Relations Act prohibits trustees from adopting a policy that will stop pension benefits if the retiree works for a nonunion employer. Ask your plan attorney and actuary for advice on stopping benefit payments for a retiree who returns to work.

7. **If an employer is delinquent in contributions, can we stop giving pension benefit and vesting credits to the employees?**

No. ERISA requires a trust to continue giving both vesting and benefit credits to the employee. The trust must also seek collection of the delinquent funds from the employer. If the employer cannot pay the delinquency, the pension credits must still be given.

Your trust attorney can advise you on the option of terminating an employer's plan participation for failure to pay contributions. Once an employer's participation is terminated, the employer has no further obligation to contribute nor do the employees have any further rights to earn benefits.

CHAPTER 6

The Audited Financial Statements

A multiemployer plan's financial statements present the monetary condition of the trust. These documents reveal the plan's income, expenses and net assets available for benefits at specific points in time as well as over time. This information is invaluable when trustees are making decisions concerning the provision of benefits and contribution levels. The reports also provide assurance to participants, contributing employers and other stakeholders that a plan has and will continue to have the resources necessary to deliver on its benefit promises.

While trustees are ultimately responsible for the preparation of plan financial statements, the actual work involved in compiling this information is delegated to the plan's administrative personnel. The statements must be prepared in accordance with generally accepted accounting principles (GAAP) as set forth by the Financial Accounting Standards Board (FASB).

Federal law requires that an independent certified public accountant (CPA) audit a multiemployer plan's financial statements annually. The auditor also has standards to follow—the American Institute of Certified Public Accountants (AICPA) auditing standards board establishes these.

The audited financial statements should provide the trustees with the following information:

- What is a general description of the plan?
- Did the plan grow or shrink during the year?
- Were there any plan amendments during the year?
- How much was paid for benefits?
- What liabilities or benefit obligations does the plan have?
- What is the most recent actuarial information?
- Does the plan have any material lease commitments, other commitments or contingent liabilities?
- What does it cost to administer the plan?
- How much does it cost to manage plan investments?
- What has been spent for property and equipment (e.g., computers, furniture)?
- How much cash is on hand?
- Are employer contributions current? How much is delinquent?
- Are collections of investment income current?
- What significant accounting policies are followed?
- What is the tax status of the plan?
- Were there any transactions with persons known to be parties in interest?
- What are the priorities in the event of plan termination?

The audited financial statements give trustees insight into administrative procedures that may need attention as well as items to discuss with other professionals. For example, a decline in the total amount of contributions may indicate a discussion with the actuary is needed on how the decline will affect pension funding. Delinquencies and the status of their collection should be reviewed with the plan attorney and administrator.

The sections that follow discuss the important parts of the audited financial statements, provide examples of what audited financial statements look like and suggest issues to consider when examining these statements. A new trustee should meet with the plan auditor to review the most recent financial statements.

Table of Contents

The table of contents directs trustees to the information included in the financial statement package.

Report of Independent Auditors

The auditor's responsibility is to express an opinion on the financial statements prepared by the plan. Thus, the report of the independent auditor is the only page of the financial statement package that actually belongs to the auditor.

Key to this report is understanding what type of opinion the auditor has given. Look for "present fairly" in the last paragraph of the report. If these two words appear without qualification, the auditor has given an *unmodified opinion* on the financial statements.

What other types of opinion might an auditor render on a plan's financial statements?

- A *qualified opinion* states that the financial statements "present fairly except for." The auditor then provides an explanation for the qualification; for example, perhaps payroll audits were not performed on contributing employers, which made it impossible for the auditor to verify plan contributions made in full.
- Another type of opinion is a *disclaimer of opinion*—The auditor is unable to give an opinion. This would be the situation if plan records had been destroyed and the auditor could not perform the audit.
- The last type of opinion is an *adverse opinion*. The auditor declares the financial statements

are not fairly presented. This might happen if plan trustees used unacceptable accounting practices in the financial statements.

If a plan has more than 100 participants, the U.S. Department of Labor (DOL) and the Internal Revenue Service (IRS) require the independent auditor's report and financial statements accompany the Form 5500 that a plan must file each year. If a plan receives anything other than an unqualified opinion from its auditor, the DOL will reject the Form 5500. The plan will be given 90 days to correct the problem(s) that resulted in the failure to get a qualified opinion. If the problem is not fixed within 90 days, monetary penalties will be assessed against the trustees of the plan.

Financial Statement for a Health and Welfare Plan

For a health and welfare plan, additions to plan assets less deductions to plan assets equals additions to net assets available for benefits. Audited financial statements have three components that provide plan trustees with information needed to assess whether this has been accomplished:

1. Statement of net assets available for benefits
2. Statement of changes in net assets available for benefits
3. Notes to the financial statement.

The *statement of net assets available for benefits* is a year-end snapshot of a plan's total assets and liabilities. It compares plan assets, liabilities and net assets available for benefits for the most recent year to the previous year. Exhibit 6-A on page 95 is an example of this statement for a health and welfare plan. Of interest to plan trustees would be these specific items in the example:

- In the previous year, all investments were in short-term funds. Investments for the current year include U.S. government and corporate bonds. Ask whether the investment policy of the plan has changed.
- Employer contributions receivable have dropped from over $5 million to less than $1.5 million. Ask the plan administrator why this decline occurred.

Exhibit 6-B on page 96 is a sample *statement of changes in net assets available for health and wel-*

Exhibit 6-A

Widget Workers' Multiemployer Health and Welfare Plan
Statement of Net Assets Available for Benefits
December 31, 2013 and 2012

	2013	2012
Assets		
Investments—at fair value		
U.S. government and government agency obligations	$ 8,719,759	$ —
Corporate bonds	9,440,512	—
Short-term investment funds	7,701,076	21,737,811
	25,861,347	21,737,811
Receivables		
Employer contributions	1,429,273	5,202,386
Prescription rebates	154,673	211,697
Accrued interest	249,174	84,479
Other	100,874	242,735
	1,933,994	5,741,297
Cash	32,262	24,342
Total Assets	27,827,603	27,503,450
Liabilities		
Accounts payable	236,876	267,588
Net Assets Available for Benefits	$27,590,727	$27,235,862

fare benefits. This report shows where the same hypothetical plan obtained its income and what its costs were. Questions to ask regarding this statement are:

- Why did employer contributions decline from $49.58 million to $44.05 million?
- Why did the contract administrator's fee increase?
- Why did actuary fees decrease by more than half?
- What is the reason for the substantial decline in the expense for postage, printing and supplies?

The auditor's *notes* typically contain:

- A description of the plan
- A summary of significant accounting policies
- A statement concerning risks and uncertainties

- A description of how plan assets are invested
- A description of any changes made to the plan documents
- A statement on plan termination language in the trust document and what happens to assets upon termination
- A note on the benefit obligations of the plan
- The tax status of the plan.

Some notes may be unique or require special explanation. For example, there might be a note that states the plan is required to pay state insurance premium taxes, the plan has a long-term lease arrangement or there is an allowance for doubtful accounts as part of income receivables. Trustees should read the notes to ensure they fully understand the financial statements. Notes also provide a brief, but helpful overview of key points concerning the plan.

Exhibit 6-B

Widget Workers' Multiemployer Health and Welfare Plan
Statement of Changes in Net Assets Available for Benefits
For the Years Ended December 31, 2013 and 2012

	2013	2012
Additions to Plan Assets Attributed to		
Contributions		
Employers	$44,055,336	$49,587,651
Participants	1,118,337	1,194,489
	45,173,673	50,782,140
Investment income		
Appreciation in fair value of investments	604,688	—
Interest income	950,603	963,633
Investment expenses	(28,484)	(3,475)
Other income	1,351	11,289
	1,528,158	971,447
Total Additions	46,701,831	51,753,587
Deductions From Plan Assets Attributed to		
Benefits	42,873,462	42,866,423
Claims administration fees	2,162,776	2,043,323
Administrative expenses		
Contract administrator fees	867,611	773,126
Legal fees	198,629	207,334
Conference and meeting expenses	7,615	6,021
Audit fees	42,268	37,855
Payroll audit fees	10,741	4,074
Hospital audits	11,830	16,550
Actuary fees	25,000	56,376
Postage, printing and supplies	76,439	131,983
Bonding and insurance	26,313	24,020
Telephone	9,614	14,393
Miscellaneous	34,668	7,710
	1,310,728	1,279,442
Total Deductions	46,346,966	46,189,188
Net Increase	354,865	5,564,399
Net Assets Available for Benefits at Beginning of Year	27,235,862	21,671,463
Net Assets Available for Benefits at End of Year	$27,590,727	$27,235,862

Financial Statement for a Defined Pension Plan

Each year, the plan actuary projects the multiemployer pension plans liability to provide future benefits. If Jack is aged 40 and has 20 years of credit in the pension plan, the actuary would predict how much the plan must have in 25 years to pay Jack's pension benefits when he retires at the age of 65.

The financial statements show trustees what the market value of plan assets are at the end of the two most recent plan years, how the assets were invested (e.g., stocks, bonds), and what plan income and expenses were. By comparing the figures in the financial statements with those in the actuary's report, trustees can determine whether plan assets are on target to meet future liabilities.

Exhibit 6-C below is an example of a *statement of net assets available for a pension benefit plan*. A review of this statement reveals:

Exhibit 6-C

Widget Workers' Multiemployer Pension Plan
Statement of Net Assets Available for Benefits
December 31, 2013 and 2012

	2013	2012
Assets		
Investments—at fair value		
U.S. government and government agency obligations	$ 7,382,785	$ 8,028,176
Corporate bonds	7,653,043	6,227,712
Foreign securities	505,511	512,000
Common stocks	21,315,679	21,605,221
Common/collective trusts	24,517,601	23,421,880
Mutual funds	9,080,679	9,035,172
Hedge funds	8,897,762	7,201,727
Pooled separate account	4,438,920	—
Short-term investment funds	1,083,158	1,244,911
	84,875,138	77,276,799
Receivables		
Employer contributions	545,698	563,312
Interest and dividends	122,390	125,333
Due from broker for investments sold	1,107,728	987,214
Other	71,725	—
	1,847,541	1,675,859
Cash	361,593	229,198
Total Assets	87,084,272	79,181,856
Liabilities		
Accounts payable	134,231	120,020
Due to broker for investments purchased	894,313	311,364
Total Liabilities	1,028,544	431,384
Net Assets Available for Benefits	$86,055,728	$78,750,472

- Plan funds are invested in nine different asset types. Ask the investment manager whether these investments are in accordance with the plan's investment guidelines including the allocation percentages set for each type of asset.

- A new investment is a pooled separate account. Ask the investment manager to explain this investment.

A sample *statement of change in net assets available for plan benefits* is presented as Exhibit 6-D below. A review of this report shows:

Exhibit 6-D

Widget Workers' Multiemployer Pension Plan
Statement of Changes in Net Assets Available for Benefits
For the Years Ended December 31, 2013 and 2012

	2013	2012
Additions to Plan Assets Attributed to		
Investment income		
Net appreciation in fair value of investments	$ 6,704,957	$ 7,397,649
Interest	939,464	857,968
Dividends	964,096	690,634
	8,608,517	8,946,251
Investment expenses	(516,181)	(401,166)
	8,092,336	8,545,085
Employer contributions	5,399,422	5,130,740
Total Additions	13,491,758	13,675,825
Deductions From Plan Assets Attributed to		
Benefits	5,314,164	4,252,120
Administrative expenses		
Contract administrator's fees	557,492	496,157
Actuarial fees	37,599	60,609
Legal fees	42,000	42,000
Audit fees	46,620	35,200
Payroll audit fees	24,452	19,885
Pension Benefit Guaranty Corporation premiums	111,704	100,573
Insurance and bonding	33,638	17,539
Printing, postage and miscellaneous	15,640	13,882
Meetings and conferences	3,193	7,845
	872,338	793,690
Total Deductions	6,186,502	5,045,810
Net Increase	7,305,256	8,630,015
Net Assets Available for Benefits at Beginning of Year	78,750,472	70,120,457
Net Assets Available for Benefits at End of Year	$86,055,728	$78,750,472

- Net appreciation in fair value of investments declined from $7.4 million last year to $6.7 million this year. Ask whether this makes sense based on what has happened in the investment markets the past two years.
- Benefits paid increased by almost 25%. Ask why this occurred and what future benefit payment increases are projected.
- There were large increases in several administrative expense categories in the past year. Ask the plan administrator to explain why these occurred.
- Legal expenses are unchanged. This suggests the plan attorney may only be used for routine matters. If this is true, consider whether the retainer may be too high.

The auditor's *notes* provide:

- A description of the plan
  - Type of plan
  - Vesting
  - Pension benefits
- A summary of accounting policies
  - How investment evaluation is made
  - How income is recognized
- The actuarial valuation
  - The assumptions (e.g., mortality, disability rate, expenses, contributions)
  - A listing of actuarial liability
- The investments
  - A listing of the assets and market values and how those market values are determined
- What happens to assets on termination
- Employer withdrawal liability
- IRS tax status and determination letter

Additional notes may address items unique to the plan and entries that require a special explanation. Read the notes to obtain a full understanding of the financial statements. Notes also offer a capsulized explanation and review of a pension plan's purpose and funding.

Common Questions and Answers

1. Our plan year is January 1 to December 31. The financial statements for last year show an investment loss of $8 million. It is now June 1, the investment manager has made up the $8 million loss and investments have gained another $6 million. Must we base financial decisions on the December 31 audit report, or can we use today's financial figures?

Financial statements are a snapshot of a plan's funding status. You should consider the year-end information, but decisions should be based on the most current figures available. If the opposite had occurred and plan assets had declined $14 million during the six months following the auditor's report, you could not make a financial decision by pretending the $14 million loss did not occur.

When making a midyear financial decision, consult with your plan auditor to be sure no significant facts have been overlooked. For example, an increase in one expense category may be offset by a decline in another expense category.

2. Another multiemployer plan wants to merge with our plan. The auditor of our plan recommends a complete audit of the other plan to provide us with financial information whether a merger is prudent. The other plan's trustees say this is an unnecessary expense and do not want to perform the audit. What should we do?

First, determine whether the other plan has annual audited financial statements. If it does, check out the reputation of the other plan's auditor. If the auditor is reputable, you can simply have your auditor update the value of the other plan's assets and liabilities as close to the merger date as possible. A complete audit may not be necessary in these circumstances.

3. The auditor's letter accompanying our plan's financial statements cites several minor bookkeeping errors. For example, the auditor cites several occasions where items are outstanding in the checking account reconciliaton for six months. The administrator says the auditor is being nitpicky and doesn't understand how difficult it is to track down some self-pay participants. What should we do?

The auditor is the professional you employ to advise you on proper financial accounting and how to manage plan assets properly. The last problem you want is imprudent handling of a cash or a checking account. There are occasions when an administrator will have problems reconciling some transactions. Let's say a participant makes a self-payment to continue medical coverage under COBRA, but the employer also reports sufficient hours to make the participant eligible for trust-paid coverage. The administrator mails the participant a reimbursement check, but the check is returned with "address unknown." This check and the reimbursement liability to the participant must be reconciled at some point. The administrator's practical solution may not be the same as the auditor's financial accounting solution.

Have the plan auditor, administrator and attorney meet to develop an acceptable procedure to follow. For example, all "stale" checks are written off after 60 days, but the administrator has the authority to issue a new check when a participant is found or comes forward within one year.

4. Our plan actuary says the actuarial report cannot be completed until the audited financial statement is final. Can we demand the auditor complete the audited financial statements as soon as possible after the end of the year plan year?

Talk with the auditor about schedules. What is the definition of *as soon as possible?* What is realistic from his or her point of view? Is the auditor held up due to reports from someone else (e.g., the custodian bank's market valuation of the assets and accounting for the receipt of interest and dividends)? Is your account low on the auditor's list of clients and priorities? As a trustee, you need to understand and evaluate the reasons for the delay.

Always make expectations, including time lines, known to all of your plan's professional advisors. If a professional cannot meet these expectations, seek the services of another competent advisor.

CHAPTER 7

Checklists for New Trustees

The checklists in this chapter are designed to be easy-to-use timesavers for you as a new trustee. The checklists summarize information from previous chapters:

- The plan documents that should be in your trustee notebook
- The professional reports you should have and what you should look for in these reports
- Information to seek from and questions to ask plan professionals when you meet them or receive a report from them at a trust meeting.

As a new trustee, you must understand the trust and plan documents, trust finances, administrative procedures and the role of the professional advisors. If you obtain the information contained in these checklists, you have taken the first step to understanding the plan you have a fiduciary duty to manage.

Multiemployer Plan Documents

Trust documents establish an employee benefit plan, dictate its operating procedures, and control the terms and conditions of benefits. Obtain a copy of the following documents:

- ☐ The provision in the collective bargaining agreement that imposes the duty on the employer(s) to participate in and contribute to the plan

- ☐ The trust agreement with all amendments
- ☐ The plan document with all amendments. Keep in mind that the plan and trust documents may be combined into one document.
- ☐ The plan booklet, also referred to as the summary plan description (SPD)
- ☐ For health plans, a copy of the summary of benefits and coverage (SBC)
- ☐ A copy of the last summary annual report (SAR) sent to participants.
- ☐ For pension plans, a copy of the annual statement sent to participants
- ☐ The investment guidelines for trust assets
- ☐ Trust meeting minutes for at least the last two years
- ☐ The fiduciary liability insurance policy covering trustees and the waiver of recourse provision
- ☐ The fidelity bond required by ERISA
- ☐ Plan procedure for collecting delinquent contributions
- ☐ Plan procedure for appealing claims
- ☐ Plan procedure for handling qualified domestic relations orders (QDROs)

These documents can be obtained from the plan administrator or attorney. Place these items in a three-ring notebook with tabs for ease in use. Keep this notebook updated and bring it to each trust meeting.

Reports From Professional Advisors

Ask the plan administrator to provide a list of all the plan's professional advisors and to identify the organizations that provide services to the plan trust such as insurance carriers, the custodian bank, HMO, PPO, etc. Also, ask for a copy of the most recent report(s) submitted to trustees by the plan administrator, plan advisors and service providers. A new trustee should review the contents of each report with the respective professional advisor or service provider. Apportion a section of a file cabinet to maintain these trust reports. Dedicate separate file folders to each subject to ensure easy access to the most recent reports and to maintain a history. In addition, obtain a copy of the following items as appropriate.

Health and Welfare Documents

- ☐ The most recent Form 5500 report filed by the plan administrator
- ☐ The financial report(s) from the plan administrator covering the most recent reporting period, the plan year to date and the past plan year
- ☐ The audited financial statements
- ☐ A summary or the report(s) on claims experience from the insurance broker or claims-paying organization for the most recent quarter, the plan or contract year to date, and the past plan year.
- ☐ The investment manager's report(s) on investment performance of trust reserves for the most recent quarter and the past plan year
- ☐ If a custodian bank is used, the bank's report for the most recent reporting period
- ☐ Copies of letters and advisory memos to trustees from the plan attorney for the past three years
- ☐ Any reports from professional advisors to trustees that pertain to retiree medical coverage
- ☐ The report on participant eligibility for the most recent reporting period. This may include hours of eligibility, vacation and holiday eligibility, hours bank, etc.

- ☐ A blank copy of the card that a participant must complete to enroll in the plan
- ☐ A blank copy of the ID card used by participants to show service providers they are plan participants
- ☐ A blank copy of the claim form(s) that participants use to file a claim
- ☐ A copy of the COBRA continuation notice sent to participants and a copy of the forms used to administer COBRA continuation coverage
- ☐ A copy of the HIPAA privacy notice

If the plan is fully insured, request:

- ☐ A copy of the insurance contract(s)
- ☐ A report from the insurance broker or insurance advisor on how the carrier contract was negotiated for the current plan year.

If the plan is self-funded, request:

- ☐ Copies of the insurance contract with the insurance carrier that provides stop-loss coverage
- ☐ A copy of the report from the professional who advises trustees on underwriting.

Pension Documents

- ☐ The most recent Form 5500 filed by the plan administrator.
- ☐ Copies of letters or advisory memos that the plan attorney has submitted to trustees over the past three years
- ☐ A blank copy of the application form completed by participants who are applying for benefits
- ☐ A blank copy of the enrollment card used by participants to enroll in the pension plan
- ☐ If a custodian bank is used, obtain the bank's report for the most current reporting period

If the plan is a defined benefit pension plan, obtain:

- ☐ The financial report(s) from the plan administrator covering the past reporting period, the plan year to date and the past plan year.
- ☐ The actuarial report from the actuary
- ☐ The audited financial statements
- ☐ Report(s) from the investment manager(s) covering the past quarter, year and five-year

period (or longest period the investment manager has worked for the plan)

If the plan has an investment consultant, request:

☐ The report(s) from the consultant covering the investment performance for the past quarter, year and five-year period (or longest period the consultant has maintained a history).

Meeting With Professional Advisors

Individuals serving as plan trustees normally have other full-time job responsibilities. In addition, they are rarely experts in the legal, auditing, actuarial, insurance, investment or administrative fields. As a result, trustees seek advice from professionals who are experts in these fields and often delegate responsibility to these professionals. The checklists above advise new trustees to obtain copies of the trust documents and reports that professional advisors have submitted to trustees. New trustees should meet informally with each of a plan's professional advisors to become familiar with the role each advisor plays. At each of these meetings, the advisor should explain the importance of the information contained in his or her report(s).

Plan Administrator and Legal Counsel

Review trust documents with both the plan administrator and legal counsel. Discuss:

☐ What is the purpose of the trust?
☐ What are the duties and powers of trustees?
☐ What are the procedures for conducting trust meetings (e.g., who can call meetings, what are the voting and quorum requirements, who keeps minutes, how many meetings are required per year)?
☐ What powers and limitations do trustees have to delegate responsibility? What is the duty of trustees to monitor the performance of those to whom duties have been delegated?
☐ What limitations exist on trustee liability? What provisions protect trustees?
☐ How are trustee costs and expenses paid?
☐ When can plan assets be used for trustee legal assistance and educational expenses?

☐ What is the plan's dispute resolution procedure and how it is applied? Has the procedure ever been used? If so, what happened?
☐ What strategies are is used to communicate with participants? Who prepares the communication? What is the procedure for trustee approval?

Other Advisors

In meetings with other plan advisors, discuss:

☐ What is the scope of services the advisor provides the trust? What is the advisor's role?
☐ What is the advisor's experience? What other qualifications does the advisor have?
☐ What reports has the advisor provided?
☐ What problems or concerns does the advisor have concerning the trust? What corrective steps are recommended?
☐ What are the strong points and positive aspects about the trust? What steps should be taken to assure these continue?
☐ What does the advisor need from trustees or other professional advisors to make the trust more efficient?
☐ What procedures, rules or policies are unique to this trust plan? What historical information can the advisor provide to support why this procedure is unique to this trust plan? How did the procedure develop?

For health and welfare plans, also ask the professional advisor:

☐ How does the experience of this plan compare to the norm?
☐ What cost-containment procedures have been initiated? Are they effective? Why or why not?
☐ What additional cost-containment procedures does the advisor recommend, and why?
☐ If the plan provides retiree coverage, what effect is the coverage having upon the plan? What are the problems, potential problems and recommended solutions?

Understanding Plan Finances and Participant Eligibility

A plan administrator is charged with the day-to-day operation of a plan. The administrator bills participating employers and collects contributions, applies participant eligibility rules, pays expenses on behalf of the trust and performs other duties as directed by trustees. During a meeting with the plan administrator, a new trustee might ask the following questions.

Employer Contributions
- [ ] When does the administrator send billings to contributing employers?
- [ ] What must the employers complete on the billing form?
- [ ] What are the codes and their significance (e.g., layoff, termination, injury)?
- [ ] Who receives employer contributions?
- [ ] How is money deposited and when does interest start accruing?
- [ ] How are employer reports processed?
- [ ] How long does it take to process a report?

Delinquency Procedures
- [ ] What happens when an employer is late or does not make a payment?
- [ ] Who processes the delinquency and what are the steps in the process?
- [ ] When does legal counsel get involved?
- [ ] What happens to participant eligibility in a delinquency situation? How are participants notified?
- [ ] What are the penalties for delinquencies? Who determines the penalties? Are the penalties ever waived?
- [ ] How are trustees informed of delinquency matters?
- [ ] Is the local union informed about employer delinquencies? Can the local union take action under the labor agreement?
- [ ] If the employer is delinquent, is there a procedure to involve the National Labor Relations Board (NLRB)?

Plan Income From Sources Other Than Contributions
- [ ] Does the plan receive income from sources other than employer contributions (e.g., investment income, participant self-payments, experience returns from insurance carriers)?

- [ ] How is additional income received and reported?

Participant Eligibility
- [ ] How is participant eligibility determined?
- [ ] Are there different types of eligibility (e.g., active, layoff, disabled, retiree)? If so, what are the eligibility requirements?
- [ ] Is there a lag month(s) system and, if so, how does it work?
- [ ] How do participants know whether they are eligible for plan benefits?
- [ ] Is there an hours bank or other continued eligibility system for participants who are not working and, if so, how does it work?
- [ ] What happens when a participant's eligibility ends? What notices are sent? How does COBRA apply?
- [ ] Are there coverage continuation and self-pay procedures for employees and dependents who lose their eligibility? If so, what are they and how do they work? What are the notice procedures?
- [ ] How is participant eligibility reported to trustees? Are statistical trends maintained?

Participation Statistics
Review participation statistics for the past month, quarter and year.
- [ ] How many participants are in each coverage category (e.g., actives, retirees, dependents, laid off, disabled)?
- [ ] If applicable, what is the number of active employees compared to the number eligible? For example, if there is a 100-hour contribution eligibility rule, what is the actual or average number who are reported with less than 100 hours, and the number reported with 100 or more hours each month?
- [ ] What statistical data on the hours bank or other continued eligibility system is available?
- [ ] What is the monthly value of the "breakage" (contributions made for noneligible employees) and how is it used?

For pension plans, also ask:
- [ ] How does the number of participants who meet the minimum service requirements

for a vesting credit each year compare with the number who do not?

☐ What is the average number of retirees each month in each retirement category (e.g., early, normal, disability) and the average benefit for retirees?

Plan Expenses

Review the plan's expenses for the past several months.

☐ What are the typical expenses of the plan?

☐ How are expenses paid? Is it necessary for trustees to approve payment of bills and expenses? If so, by whom and when, and what is the procedure?

Plan Assets and Reserves

For health and welfare plans, ask:

☐ If contribution cash flow does not meet expenses, what funding source is used to make up the shortfall?

☐ What type of reserve account(s) does the plan have?

☐ What is the purpose of each reserve account?

☐ How is the amount of the reserve determined?

☐ What is the current amount in each reserve account?

☐ How and when are payments made out of reserves?

☐ If a payment is made out of a reserve account, how are the funds replaced?

☐ What are the investment guidelines for reserves? Who establishes the guidelines?

☐ Who makes investment decisions?

☐ Who monitors investment performance?

☐ What is the history of investment performance?

☐ Who is responsible for payment of interest and dividends? Who suffers the loss for late dividend payments?

For defined benefit pension plans, ask:

☐ What resources are used to pay pension benefits and plan expenses?

☐ If contribution cash flow exceeds benefit and expense payments, how is the excess allocated to the investment manager(s)?

☐ If contribution cash flow is less than benefit and expense payments, what plan assets cover the shortfall?

☐ What are the investment guidelines for plan assets? Who establishes the guidelines?

☐ Who makes investment decisions?

☐ How is investment performance monitored?

☐ What has been the investment performance for the past quarter, year and three-year period?

☐ Who monitors investment transaction fees? How are they accounted for?

☐ How is investment return accounted for?

☐ Who is responsible for payment of interest and dividends? Who suffers the loss for late dividend or interest payments?

For a defined contribution pension plan:

☐ How is investment return posted to an individual's account? How often?

☐ What is done upon retirement to close an individual's account?

Understanding Benefit Procedures

The purpose of the employee benefit plan is to provide benefits for eligible participants and their beneficiaries. The plan document and summary plan description (SPD) provide the eligibility requirements and benefit levels. These documents also explain the administrative procedures a participant must follow to apply for and receive benefits. The new trustee should meet with the person or organization that is responsible for payment of benefits (claims payer) to learn how the benefit application and payment procedures work.

Plan Enrollment

☐ How are enrollment cards distributed to new plan participants? Who is responsible for distribution of the cards?

☐ How is the completed enrollment card returned to the administrator?

☐ What does the administrator do with the completed enrollment card?

☐ What are the checks to ensure the accuracy of the data on the enrollment card?

☐ What are the checks to eliminate benefit fraud? For example, how does the plan verify dependents are really dependents?

- [ ] What are the strengths and weaknesses of the enrollment process and what can be done to improve it?

Benefit Application

- [ ] How does the participant apply for benefits (e.g., complete an application form, show an identification card)?
- [ ] Are there any conditions or limitations on benefits (e.g., a health and welfare plan may require the use of a PPO hospital/physician/pharmacy, precertification and a second opinion; a pension plan may have limitations on age or length of service)?
- [ ] What happens if a participant does not follow the proper application procedure? Are there penalties?
- [ ] For health and welfare benefits, how long after receiving treatment may a participant submit a claim and have it paid?
- [ ] For pension benefits, what documents must a participant submit in addition to the application form (e.g., birth certificate, marriage license)?
- [ ] For life insurance benefits, what documents must be filed (e.g., death certificate)?

Benefit Payment

- [ ] For a health and welfare plan, who receives the payment? Is it the participant or the provider (e.g., doctor, hospital)? How is a participant informed if a payment is made directly to the provider?
- [ ] For pension benefits, what are the benefit payment options and how does a participant select an option?
- [ ] For pension and life insurance benefits, who receives payment after the death of a participant? How is the right of payment determined? What if there is a dispute? Is there a plan rule that determines payment in the event the participant does not have a designated beneficiary?
- [ ] What is the process for notifying a participant about required income taxes on benefits and the option to withhold the tax payment from the benefit?
- [ ] What is the benefit appeal procedure and how does it work?

Summary

As a new trustee, if you follow the checklists outlined above, you will obtain most of the information needed to intelligently participate in discussions at trust meetings and make responsible decisions. The educational process, however, is ongoing. A trustee has fiduciary responsibilities and must continue to be actively involved in communicating with plan professional advisors on a regular basis, reviewing reports and monitoring performance.

Appendix

Know Your Numbers Wellness Program
by Lorie Shorett and Joe Brislin

*K*now Your Numbers can be used by multi-employer plans and plan sponsors as an easy, low-cost first step to a wellness program or an addition to an ongoing program. The endeavor is intended to encourage participants to know and understand what their personal numbers are for blood pressure, good and bad cholesterol, blood glucose and body mass. These numbers substantially affect a person's health and ability to work and enjoy life. They also impact the claims costs of health plans.

Trustees or plan sponsors normally understand why a wellness program is beneficial to both a health plan and the plan participants. However, they may also be concerned about the scope of the program, its cost, acceptance by plan participants and/or lack of objective evidence that the proposed program will actually produce the desired results. Discussed below, *Know Your Numbers* is an easy-to-understand and easy-to-implement wellness program that can provide positive results for a health plan and plan participants.

Why Wellness?

Professional consultants have advised trustees and plan sponsors that a wellness program will benefit plan participants, the claims costs of the health plan and the overall productivity of the company. For example, the American Heart Association states a plan can save $16 for every $1 invested in health and wellness.

A 2009 "Health Care Trends in America" study by Blue Cross Blue Shield of America calculated the following 2007 costs for the U.S. workforce:

Condition	Lost Work Days	Lost Productivity
Diabetes	12.5 million	$2.1 billion
Heart Disease	6.3 million	$1.0 billion
Hypertension	12.3 million	$2.0 billion

A study published in the April 2009 issue of the *Journal of Occupational and Environmental Medicine* found that for every dollar spent for claims in a medical plan, there is a $2.30 of health-related productivity loss to the employer due to absenteeism and presenteeism. The study found that an employee present on the job but not performing at full productive capacity (*presenteeism*) was actually more costly than being absent from work.

The cost drivers for both medical costs and productivity losses include diabetes, back and neck pain, coronary heart disease, chronic pain, high cholesterol, depression, obesity and anxiety. Each of these cost drivers is related to the person's health and lifestyle. The four *Know Your Numbers* tests are for blood pressure, blood glucose, cholesterol and body mass index, which function as indicators of medical claim cost drivers.

The U.S. Centers for Disease Control and Prevention estimate 66% of U.S. adults are overweight or obese. Weight has a price tag. Overweight people are more prone to back pain, heart disease, stroke, diabetes and some forms of cancer. Humana of New York published a study that shows the average annual health care cost is $534 for the overweight and $1,614 for the obese. The *Archives of Internal Medicine* published a report showing overweight and obese people had 13 times higher lost work days, filed twice as many workers' compensation claims and had seven times higher medical costs for workers' compensation.

A *Know Your Numbers* campaign will not immediately reduce health care costs or lost productivity. It is designed to be a first step to make plan participants aware that their personal numbers affect their lives and it is not difficult to obtain their numbers. The intent of the program is to lead a plan participant and his or her doctor into discussion of information and to create ongoing awareness. Instead of the physician just performing the procedures to determine the numbers and entering them into the patient's file, *Know Your Numbers* encourages the physician and patient to examine the numbers and what they mean to the patient. The wallet cards will remind the participant to continue the dialog with each visit to the physician.

Implementing the Program

The Bledsoe Health Trust is a multiemployer plan that provides health coverage for forest products workers, retirees and dependents in five northwestern states. It is cosponsored by the Carpenters Industrial Council (CIC) and TOC Management Services. Rita Sickler from Regence Blue Cross of Oregon and Laurie Shorett, editor of the quarterly *Bledsoe Health Trust* newsletter, worked with the trustee technical committee to develop the *Know Your Numbers* information sheet at the end of this appendix along with the wallet card. The *Know Your Numbers* insert was included in a quarterly newsletter sent to all active and retiree plan participants. The local union representatives and company human resource managers also helped promote the program.

Other Options

Other options that trustees and plan sponsors can include in a *Know Your Numbers* campaign can increase effectiveness but will add to the cost and administration. These are:

- Schedule procedures and tests at a company location, local clinic, health fair, etc. to make participation easier.
- A coordination or tie-in with a disease management or case management cost-containment program
- Cash, prize incentives or a waiver of co-pays or deductibles for plan participants who make an office visit for the numbers tests and procedures within the first three to six months of the campaign.

Summary

Trustees and plan sponsors should not underestimate the total costs of health for the individual participant, the health plan and a company's overall productivity. Wellness programs can decrease costs and increase productivity. The *Know Your Numbers* program can be a start of a wellness program that is easy to understand and implement.

Wallet Card:
Know Your Numbers Insert

Knowing your numbers is the most important thing you can do to protect your good health and reduce your risk of costly health problems. There are four key health measurements that are good indicators of future health: cholesterol, blood pressure, body mass index (BMI) and blood sugar. To make it easy for you to know your numbers, Regence has created a wallet card so you can record and track your results.

High cholesterol increases your chance of heart disease, and may not cause symptoms at first. **All** healthy adults over the age of 20 should have a blood test called a "fasting lipid profile" test at least once every five years. This test will reveal your total cholesterol, LDL (bad) cholesterol, HDL (good) cholesterol and triglyceride levels.

Many people don't know they have high blood pressure, because there usually aren't any symptoms. Left untreated, high blood pressure can lead to serious problems such as heart attack, stroke, blindness and kidney failure. **All** healthy adults should have their blood pressure checked at every doctor appointment, or at least every two years.

Being overweight and obese leads to many health problems, such as high blood pressure, heart disease, diabetes, stroke, arthritis and breathing disorders. You are less likely to have health problems if you maintain a healthy weight. Check with your doctor to see how often you should have a full checkup, including height and weight.

Diabetes can affect your whole body. When your blood sugar is too high for too long, it can lead to problems with your heart, blood vessels, eyes and kidneys. **All** healthy adults over the age of 45 should have a blood glucose test every three years.

If you have other risk factors, ask your doctor how often you should have these tests— you might need to be checked more often.

How Does It Work?

Take your wallet card to every doctor appointment, and record your numbers on it. Ask your doctor what your personal goals should be and what any changes in your numbers might mean. If you're overweight, talk with your doctor about the effect BMI has on your health and increased risk of disease.

Knowing and tracking your numbers over time will allow you to gauge your risk for diabetes, heart disease and stroke. And, it will help you focus on making the lifestyle changes that matter most, such as tobacco cessation, getting more exercise or eating right.

Tips to Improve Overall Health
- Enjoy 30-60 minutes of physical activity on most days of the week.
- Don't smoke cigarettes or use other tobacco products.
- Limit your alcohol intake.
- Know what your weight should be and keep it at or below that level.
- Cut back on foods high in saturated fats or cholesterol.
- Eat at least five servings of fruits and vegetables each day.

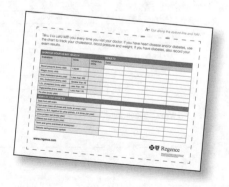

Knowing your numbers is essential to your quest for better health. Here are some more ways to improve your medical condition.

Improve Your Heart Health

- Enjoy 30-60 minutes of physical activity on most days of the week.
- Take your medicine exactly as prescribed; don't run out of pills even for a single day.
- Don't smoke cigarettes or use other tobacco products.
- Ask your doctor about taking aspirin to help prevent heart attack and stroke.
- Limit your alcohol intake.
- Know what your weight should be and keep it at or below that level.
- Know your blood pressure and have it checked regularly.
- Keep appointments with your doctor.

Lower Your Cholesterol

- Cut back on foods high in saturated fats and cholesterol.
- Eat at least five servings of fruits and vegetables daily.

Lower Your Blood Pressure

- Limit your intake of salty foods.
- Eat five or more servings of fruits and vegetables each day. Include a few servings of fat-free or low-fat dairy products.

✂ *Cut along the dotted line and fold .*

Take this card with you every time you visit your doctor. If you have heart disease and/or diabetes, use the chart to track your cholesterol, blood pressure and weight. If you have diabetes, also record your exam results.

MONITOR YOUR HEART HEALTH			RESULTS			
Evaluations	GOAL	PERSONAL GOAL	Dates			
Blood pressure (every visit)	130/80					
Weight (every visit)						
Total cholesterol (every year)	Less than 200					
HDL cholesterol (every year)	Greater than 40					
LDL cholesterol (every year)	Less than 100					
Triglycerides (every year)	Less than 150					
Flu shot (every year)						
MONITOR YOUR DIABETES						
Daily foot self-exam						
Foot exam (take off shoes and socks at every visit)						
HbA1c (< 8.0, negative for urine protein, 2-4 times per year)						
Urine protein test (every year)						
Dilated eye exam (every year)						
Teeth and gums examined (2 times/year)						
Diabetic eating/exercise update						

www.regence.com

Regence BlueCross BlueShield of Oregon and Regence Life and Health Insurance Company are Independent Licensees of the Blue Cross and Blue Shield Association

Together, we can take cha

Index

A

B

Basis points, 60
Benefit credits, 36, 41, 46
Benefit eligibility, 77-78, 88, 102, 104
    determining, 81-82, 104
    health and welfare plans, 20-21, 81-82
    hours-based, 80-81
    pension plans, 45-49, 84-85
    rules, 8, 80-81, 104
    waiting periods, 80
Benefit payments, 7-8, 10-11, 22-26, 29,
    83-85
    actuarial reductions, 47-48
    application for, 78, 106
    coordination of, 84
    health and welfare, 15, 22-26, 29, 63, 83-84,
      90-91
    pension, 37, 41, 47-49, 84-85, 106
    see also claims (Health benefit) *and* Joint and
      survivor option
Benefits statement, 12
Beta, 64-65
Bond indexes, 62-63, 67, 71
bond, Fidelity, 7, 14-15, 78, 88, 101
Bonds, 58-59, 71
    duration of, 60, 64
    maturity, 58-59
    ratings, 58-59
Breakage, 79, 104
Brock v. Henderschott, 5

C

Capital appreciation, 65
Case management, 25
Cash equivalents, 59
claims, Health benefit, 83-84
    administrator as payer of, 83-84, 90-91
    appeals, 8, 12, 29, 78, 85-88, 101, 106
    audit, 29
    denial of, 8, 12, 78, 85-86
    experience, 102
    experience refund, 27
    form, 102
    limits on, 22-26
    payment of, 29, 83-84
    risk, 28, 31
    see also Benefit payments
Claims-made policy, 15
Claims payer, 83-84, 90-91
Clinical trials, 24
Closed panel service providers, 26
COBRA. *See* Consolidated Omnibus Budget
    Reconciliation Act of 1985 (COBRA)
Coinsurance, 22-23
Collecting contributions. *See* Contributions and
    payments
Collective bargaining, 15
    underfunded pension plans and, 40-41
Collective bargaining agreement, 2, 8, 10, 15,
    37, 78, 101
Communication with participants, 12, 33,
    77-79, 85, 87-88, 103
    see also Summary plan description (SPD)
confidentiality. *See* Health Insurance Portability
    and Accountability Act (HIPAA)
compliance, Legal, 79, 88
    checklist, 88
Consolidated Omnibus Budget Reconcilia-
    tion Act (COBRA) of 1985, 12, 21-22, 27,
    32, 78, 80, 102, 104
    notices, 12, 82, 102

Consumer Price Index (CPI), 72

Continuation of health coverage. *See* Consolidated Omnibus Budget Reconciliation Act of 1985 (COBRA)

Contract bids, 5, 9

Contrarian manager, 65

Contributions and payments, 1-2, 8, 27, 37, 104
  collection of, 11-12, 15-16, 77-79, 87, 93, 104
  contribution rates, 1, 8, 10, 15
  monitoring, 82
  policy and procedures, 11, 27
  reporting, 82, 87
  see also Delinquent contributions and payments

Coordination of benefits (COB), 84

Copayments, 23

Core manager, 65

Cosmetic surgery. *See* Medically necessary vs. unnecessary procedures

Custodian bank, 14, 27, 68, 102

D

Death benefits, 36-41, 48-49, 81-82, 85, 106
  nonspouse beneficiaries, 37

Decision deadlock, 2, 4-5, 7

Defined benefit plans, 37-42, 50-51
  actuarial assumptions, 40, 47, 51-52, 57, 72
  actuarial reduction of benefits, 47-48
  advantages and disadvantages, 41-42, 50-51
  De minimis rule, 42
  funding, 33, 37-41
  investment risk (participant), 41
  overfunded plans, 33
  payout options, 52, 85, 106
  underfunded plans, 40-41
  vesting, 36, 45-46, 52
  withdrawal liability of employers, 8, 42-43, 49, 51
  see also Pension plans

Defined contribution plans, 42-44
  advantages and disadvantages, 43-44, 50-51
  employee loans, 43, 84
  fee disclosure, 83
  funding, 42-43
  hardship withdrawals, 43
  investment risk (participant), 43-44
  payout options, 84
  See also Pension plans

Deidentification process, 31

Delinquent contributions and payments, 2, 15-16, 27, 79, 87
  policies and procedures, 8, 11-12, 87, 101, 104
  termination of benefits, 27, 33, 91-92

De minimis rule, 42

Department of Labor (DOL), 5, 9, 44, 50
  audit, 9, 50
  auditor's report and, 94
  authority of, 5
  claim appeals, 86

Disability retirement, 48, 85

Disease management, 25

Dispute resolution, 2, 4-5

Divorced spouses, 36-37

DOL. *See* Department of Labor (DOL)

Dole v. Formica, 5, 89

Donavan v. Daugherty, 6

Donavan v. Tricario, 6

E

F

G

Gainful employment, 48
Generally accepted accounting principles (GAAP), 93
Generic drugs v. brand-name drugs, 23
Genetic Information and Nondiscrimination Act (GINA), 31
Gilliam v. Edwards, 89
Global investments, 58, 71
Global macro strategy, 66
Grandfathered health plans, 23
Green zone, 40-41
Growth manager, 65
Guaranteed investment contracts (GICs), 59

H

Health and welfare plans, 19-34
  benchmark plans, 23
  benefit types, 1, 22-23
  case management, 25
  continuation of coverage, 89-90. *See also* Consolidated Omnibus Reconciliation Act of 1985 (COBRA) *and* Hours bank
  cost-containment, 22-26, 33
  coverage limits and exclusions, 23-25
  definition of, 3
  expenses, 27
  experimental procedures, 23-24
  financing, 27-28
  government mandates, 23
  grandfathered plans, 23
  income, 27
  medically unnecessary procedures, 23-24
  nonunit employees, 21
  participants, categories of, 20-21
  plan design, 20-26
  plan enrollment, 81-82
  preauthorization, 25
  prevention and wellness, 25-26
  reserves, 27, 33-34, 72-73, 105
  termination of benefits, 33
  self- vs. fully insured, 28, 31
  service providers, 26-27, 78
  see also Administration, Application for benefits, Benefit eligibility, Benefit payments, claims (Health benefit), Contributions and payments, Enrollment of participants, Fiduciary duties and responsibilities, Health Insurance Portability and Accountability Act (HIPAA), Plan advisors, Plan finances/funding *and* Service providers
Health Insurance Portability and Accountability Act (HIPAA), 29-31, 79, 102
  aggregate health information, 31
  deidentification process, 31
  protected health information (PHI), 30-31
Health maintenance organization (HMO), 14, 26, 28-29
Hours bank, 21-22, 31-32, 104

M

N

O

P

R

Real estate indexes, 62, 67, 71
Real estate investment, 59, 71, 74-75
Real rate of return, 72
Reciprocity, 49, 77, 83
Red zone, 41
Rehabilitation plan, 41
Relative value strategy, 66
Reported participants, 79
Required written agreement, 2
Reserves, Health and welfare plan, 27, 33-34,
　72-73, 105
　restricted, 27, 33-34
　unrestricted, 27, 34
Retirees, 36
　medical coverage and tax withholdng, 85
　working retirees, 91
Retirement
　disability retirement, 48
　early retirement, 47-48
　normal retirement, 47
Retirment plans. *See* Pension plans
Retirement Equity Act (REA), 36

S

SBC. *See* Summary of benefits and coverage
Secondary payer, 84
Sector rotator manager, 65
Securities and Exchange Commission (SEC),
　69
Self-funded plan. *See* Self-insurance
Self-insurance, 28, 31, 102
Self-payments, 27
Service providers
　closed panel, 26
　open panel, 26
　selection of, 78
Shareholders,
　prohibited transactions, 5
Sixty-Five Security Plan v. Blue Cross, 6
Social investing, 74-75
Sole and exclusive benefit, 1, 3
SPD. *See* Summary plan description (SPD)
specialty drugs, Coverage of, 24
Spousal consent form, 36
Statement of changes in net assets available
　for benefits
　health and welfare plans, 94-96
　pension plans, 97-99
Statement of net assets available for benefits
　health and welfare plans, 94-96
　pension plans, 97-99
Stock indexes, 62-63, 67, 71, 78
Stocks, 58, 70-71
Stop-loss insurance, 28
Summary annual report, 12, 82-83, 101
Summary of benefits and coverage, 12, 20,
　27, 80-81
　dissemination of, 20, 81
　format of, 20
　self-payments and the, 27

U

Underfunded pension plans, 40-42
Unfunded vested liability, 49
**Uniformed Services Employment and
    Reemployment Rights Act (USERRA)
    of 1994,** 10, 12, 27, 46, 82
Unit work, 45
Usual customary rates (UCR), 26

V

Value manager, 66
Vesting, 36, 45-46, 52
    and delinquent contributions, 92
    terminated nonvested participants, 36, 42
    terminated vested participants, 36
    see also Reciprocity
Volatility, 61-62

W

Waiver of recourse, 6, 14
Withdrawal liability of employers, 8, 42-43,
    49, 51
Written agreement. *See* Required written
    agreement

Y

Yellow zone, 41